GENOCIDE & PERSECUTION

# Kosovo

# Titles in the Genocide and Persecution Series

# GENOCIDE & PERSECUTION

# | Kosovo

**Noah Berlatsky**
*Book Editor*

**Frank Chalk**
*Consulting Editor*

**GREENHAVEN PRESS**
*A part of Gale, Cengage Learning*

GALE
CENGAGE Learning·

Detroit • New York • San Francisco • New Haven, Conn • Waterville, Maine • London

Elizabeth Des Chenes, *Director, Publishing Solutions*

© 2013 Greenhaven Press, a part of Gale, Cengage Learning

Gale and Greenhaven Press are registered trademarks used herein under license.

For more information, contact:
Greenhaven Press
27500 Drake Rd.
Farmington Hills, MI 48331-3535
Or you can visit our Internet site at gale.cengage.com.

For product information and technology assistance, contact us at:

Gale Customer Support, 1-800-877-4253
For permission to use material from this text or product, submit all requests online at www.cengage.com/permissions

Further permissions questions can be emailed to permissionrequest@cengage.com

Every effort is made to ensure that Greenhaven Press accurately reflects the original intent of the authors. Every effort has been made to trace the owners of copyrighted material.

Cover image © Imagestate Media Partners Limited-Impact Photos/Alamy.
Interior barbed wire artwork © f9photos, used under license from Shutterstock.com.

**LIBRARY OF CONGRESS CATALOGING-IN-PUBLICATION DATA**

Kosovo / Noah Berlatsky, book editor.
    p. cm. -- (Genocide and persecution)
    Includes bibliographical references and index.
    ISBN 978-0-7377-6255-6 (hardcover)
    1. Kosovo War, 1998–1999--Atrocities. 2. Yugoslav War, 1991–1995--Atrocities.
3. Genocide--Serbia--Kosovo--History--20th century. 4. Albanians--Crimes against--
Serbia--Kosovo. 5. Serbs--Crimes against--Serbia--Kosovo. I. Berlatsky, Noah.
    DR2087.6.A76K67 2012
    949.7103'154--dc23
                                                      2012014593

Printed in the United States of America
1 2 3 4 5 6 7 16 15 14 13 12

# Contents

A human rights website argues that Serb atrocities against Albanians constituted gendercide (gender-selective mass killings) and genocide.

A former Canadian Parliament member argues that Canada violated its traditional role as peacemaker by participating in the aggressive NATO war against Serbia.

## Chapter 3: Personal Narratives

# Preface

> *"For the dead and the living, we must bear witness."*
>
> *Elie Wiesel, Nobel laureate and Holocaust survivor*

The histories of many nations are shaped by horrific events involving torture, violent repression, and systematic mass killings. The inhumanity of such events is difficult to comprehend, yet understanding why such events take place, what impact they have on society, and how they may be prevented in the future is vitally important. The Genocide and Persecution series provides readers with anthologies of previously published materials on acts of genocide, crimes against humanity, and other instances of extreme persecution, with an emphasis on events taking place in the twentieth and twenty-first centuries. The series offers essential historical background on these significant events in modern world history, presents the issues and controversies surrounding the events, and provides first-person narratives from people whose lives were altered by the events. By providing primary sources, as well as analysis of crucial issues, these volumes help develop critical-thinking skills and support global connections. In addition, the series directly addresses curriculum standards focused on informational text and literary nonfiction and explicitly promotes literacy in history and social studies.

Each Genocide and Persecution volume focuses on genocide, crimes against humanity, or severe persecution. Material from a variety of primary and secondary sources presents a multinational perspective on the event. Articles are carefully edited and introduced to provide context for readers. The series includes volumes on significant and widely studied events like the Holocaust, as well as events that are less often studied, such as the East Pakistan genocide in what is now Bangladesh. Some volumes focus on multiple events endured by a specific people, such as the Kurds, or multiple events enacted over time by a particular oppressor or in a particular location, such as the People's Republic of China.

Each volume is organized into three chapters. The first chapter provides readers with general background information and uses primary sources such as testimony from tribunals or international courts, documents or speeches from world leaders, and legislative text. The second chapter presents multinational perspectives on issues and controversies and addresses current implications or long-lasting effects of the event. Viewpoints explore such topics as root causes; outside interventions, if any; the impact on the targeted group and the region; and the contentious issues that arose in the aftermath. The third chapter presents first-person narratives from affected people, including survivors, family members of victims, perpetrators, officials, aid workers, and other witnesses.

In addition, numerous features are included in each volume of Genocide and Persecution:

- An annotated **table of contents** provides a brief summary of each essay in the volume.
- A **foreword** gives important background information on the recognition, definition, and study of genocide in recent history and examines current efforts focused on the prevention of future atrocities.
- A **chronology** offers important dates leading up to, during, and following the event.
- **Primary sources**—including historical newspaper accounts, testimony, and personal narratives—are among the varied selections in the anthology.
- **Illustrations**—including a world map, photographs, charts, graphs, statistics, and tables—are closely tied

to the text and chosen to help readers understand key points or concepts.

- **Sidebars**—including biographies of key figures and overviews of earlier or related historical events—offer additional content.
- **Pedagogical features**—including analytical exercises, writing prompts, and group activities—introduce each chapter and help reinforce the material. These features promote proficiency in writing, speaking, and listening skills and literacy in history and social studies.
- A **glossary** defines key terms, as needed.
- An annotated list of international **organizations to contact** presents sources of additional information on the volume topic.
- A **list of primary source documents** provides an annotated list of reports, treaties, resolutions, and judicial decisions related to the volume topic.
- A **for further research** section offers a bibliography of books, periodical articles, and Internet sources and an annotated section of other items such as films and websites.
- A comprehensive subject **index** provides access to key people, places, events, and subjects cited in the text.

The Genocide and Persecution series illuminates atrocities that cannot and should not be forgotten. By delving deeply into these events from a variety of perspectives, students and other readers are provided with the information they need to think critically about the past and its implications for the future.

# Foreword

The term *genocide* often appears in news stories and other literature. It is not widely known, however, that the core meaning of the term comes from a legal definition, and the concept became part of international criminal law only in 1951 when the United Nations Convention on the Prevention and Punishment of the Crime of Genocide came into force. The word *genocide* appeared in print for the first time in 1944 when Raphael Lemkin, a Polish Jewish refugee from Adolf Hitler's World War II invasion of Eastern Europe, invented the term and explored its meaning in his pioneering book *Axis Rule in Occupied Europe*.

## Humanity's Recognition of Genocide and Persecution

Lemkin understood that throughout the history of the human race there have always been leaders who thought they could solve their problems not only through victory in war, but also by destroying entire national, ethnic, racial, or religious groups. Such annihilations of entire groups, in Lemkin's view, deprive the world of the very cultural diversity and richness in languages, traditions, values, and practices that distinguish the human race from all other life on earth. Genocide is not only unjust, it threatens the very existence and progress of human civilization, in Lemkin's eyes.

Looking to the past, Lemkin understood that the prevailing coarseness and brutality of earlier human societies and the lower value placed on human life obscured the existence of genocide. Sacrifice and exploitation, as well as torture and public execution, had been common at different times in history. Looking toward a more humane future, Lemkin asserted the need to punish—and when possible prevent—a crime for which there had been no name until he invented it.

## Legal Definitions of Genocide

On December 9, 1948, the United Nations adopted its Convention on the Prevention and Punishment of the Crimes of Genocide (UNGC). Under Article II, genocide

> means any of the following acts committed with intent to destroy, in whole or in part, a national, ethnical, racial or religious group, as such:
>
> (a) Killing members of the group;
> (b) Causing serious bodily or mental harm to members of the group;
> (c) Deliberately inflicting on the group conditions of life calculated to bring about its physical destruction in whole or in part;
> (d) Imposing measures intended to prevent births within the group;
> (e) Forcibly transferring children of the group to another group.

Article III of the Convention defines the elements of the crime of genocide, making punishable:

> (a) Genocide;
> (b) Conspiracy to commit genocide;
> (c) Direct and public incitement to commit genocide;
> (d) Attempt to commit genocide;
> (e) Complicity in genocide.

After intense debate, the architects of the Convention excluded acts committed with intent to destroy social, political, and economic groups from the definition of genocide. Thus, attempts to destroy whole social classes—the physically and mentally challenged, and homosexuals, for example—are not acts of genocide under the terms of the UNGC. These groups achieved a belated but very significant measure of protection under international criminal law in the Rome Statute of the International Criminal

Court, adopted at a conference on July 17, 1998, and entered into force on July 1, 2002.

The Rome Statute defined a crime against humanity in the following way:

> any of the following acts when committed as part of a widespread and systematic attack directed against any civilian population:
>
> (a) Murder;
>
> (b) Extermination;
>
> (c) Enslavement;
>
> (d) Deportation or forcible transfer of population;
>
> (e) Imprisonment or other severe deprivation of physical liberty in violation of fundamental rules of international law;
>
> (f) Torture;
>
> (g) Rape, sexual slavery, enforced prostitution, forced pregnancy, enforced sterilization, or any other form of sexual violence of comparable gravity;
>
> (h) Persecution against any identifiable group or collectivity on political, racial, national, ethnic, cultural, religious, gender . . . or other grounds that are universally recognized as impermissible under international law, in connection with any act referred to in this paragraph or any crime within the jurisdiction of this Court;
>
> (i) Enforced disappearance of persons;
>
> (j) The crime of apartheid;
>
> (k) Other inhumane acts of a similar character intentionally causing great suffering, or serious injury to body or to mental or physical health.

Although genocide is often ranked as "the crime of crimes," in practice prosecutors find it much easier to convict perpetrators of crimes against humanity rather than genocide under domestic laws. However, while Article I of the UNGC declares that countries adhering to the UNGC recognize genocide as "a crime under international law which they undertake to prevent and to punish," the Rome Statute provides no comparable international mechanism for the prosecution of crimes against humanity. A treaty would help individual countries and international institutions introduce measures to prevent crimes against humanity, as well as open more avenues to the domestic and international prosecution of war criminals.

## The Evolving Laws of Genocide

In the aftermath of the serious crimes committed against civilians in the former Yugoslavia since 1991 and the Rwanda genocide of 1994, the United Nations Security Council created special international courts to bring the alleged perpetrators of these events to justice. While the UNGC stands as the standard definition of genocide in law, the new courts contributed significantly to today's nuanced meaning of genocide, crimes against humanity, ethnic cleansing, and serious war crimes in international criminal law.

Also helping to shape contemporary interpretations of such mass atrocity crimes are the special and mixed courts for Sierra Leone, Cambodia, Lebanon, and Iraq, which may be the last of their type in light of the creation of the International Criminal Court (ICC), with its broad jurisdiction over mass atrocity crimes in all countries that adhere to the Rome Statute of the ICC. The Yugoslavia and Rwanda tribunals have already clarified the law of genocide, ruling that rape can be prosecuted as a weapon in committing genocide, evidence of intent can be absent when convicting low-level perpetrators of genocide, and public incitement to commit genocide is a crime even if genocide does not immediately follow the incitement.

Several current controversies about genocide are worth noting and will require more research in the future:

1. Dictators accused of committing genocide or persecution may hold onto power more tightly for fear of becoming

vulnerable to prosecution after they step down. Therefore, do threats of international indictments of these alleged perpetrators actually delay transfers of power to more representative rulers, thereby causing needless suffering?

2. Would the large sum of money spent for international retributive justice be better spent on projects directly benefiting the survivors of genocide and persecution?

3. Can international courts render justice impartially or do they deliver only "victors' justice," that is the application of one set of rules to judge the vanquished and a different and laxer set of rules to judge the victors?

It is important to recognize that the law of genocide is constantly evolving, and scholars searching for the roots and early warning signs of genocide may prefer to use their own definitions of genocide in their work. While the UNGC stands as the standard definition of genocide in law, the debate over its interpretation and application will never end. The ultimate measure of the value of any definition of genocide is its utility for identifying the roots of genocide and preventing future genocides.

## Motives for Genocide and Early Warning Signs

When identifying past cases of genocide, many scholars work with some version of the typology of motives published in 1990 by historian Frank Chalk and sociologist Kurt Jonassohn in their book *The History and Sociology of Genocide*. The authors identify the following four motives and acknowledge that they may overlap, or several lesser motives might also drive a perpetrator:

1. To eliminate a real or potential threat, as in Imperial Rome's decision to annihilate Carthage in 146 BC.

2. To spread terror among real or potential enemies, as in Genghis Khan's destruction of city-states and people who rebelled against the Mongols in the thirteenth century.

3. To acquire economic wealth, as in the case of the Massachusetts Puritans' annihilation of the native Pequot people in 1637.

4. To implement a belief, theory, or an ideology, as in the case of Germany's decision under Hitler and the Nazis to destroy completely the Jewish people of Europe from 1941 to 1945.

Although these motives represent differing goals, they share common early warning signs of genocide. A good example of genocide in recent times that could have been prevented through close attention to early warning signs was the genocide of 1994 inflicted on the people labeled as "Tutsi" in Rwanda. Between 1959 and 1963, the predominantly Hutu political parties in power stigmatized all Tutsi as members of a hostile racial group, violently forcing their leaders and many civilians into exile in neighboring countries through a series of assassinations and massacres. Despite systematic exclusion of Tutsi from service in the military, government security agencies, and public service, as well as systematic discrimination against them in higher education, hundreds of thousands of Tutsi did remain behind in Rwanda. Government-issued cards identified each Rwandan as Hutu or Tutsi.

A generation later, some Tutsi raised in refugee camps in Uganda and elsewhere joined together, first organizing politically and then militarily, to reclaim a place in their homeland. When the predominantly Tutsi Rwanda Patriotic Front invaded Rwanda from Uganda in October 1990, extremist Hutu political parties demonized all of Rwanda's Tutsi as traitors, ratcheting up hate propaganda through radio broadcasts on government-run Radio Rwanda and privately owned radio station RTLM. Within the print media, *Kangura* and other publications used vicious cartoons to further demonize Tutsi and to stigmatize any Hutu who dared advocate bringing Tutsi into the government. Massacres of dozens and later hundreds of Tutsi sprang up even as Rwandans prepared to elect a coalition government led by moderate political parties, and as the United Nations dispatched a small international military force led by Canadian general Roméo Dallaire to oversee the elections and political transition. Late in 1992, an international human rights organization's investigating team detected the hate propaganda campaign, verified systematic massacres of Tutsi, and warned the international community that Rwanda had already entered the early stages of genocide, to no avail. On April 6, 1994, Rwanda's genocidal killing accelerated at an alarming pace when someone shot down the airplane flying Rwandan president Juvenal Habyarimana home from peace talks in Arusha, Tanzania.

Hundreds of thousands of Tutsi civilians—including children, women, and the elderly—died horrible deaths because the world ignored the early warning signs of the genocide and refused to act. Prominent among those early warning signs were: 1) systematic, government-decreed discrimination against the Tutsi as members of a supposed racial group; 2) government-issued identity cards labeling every Tutsi as a member of a racial group; 3) hate propaganda casting all Tutsi as subversives and traitors; 4) organized assassinations and massacres targeting Tutsi; and 5) indoctrination of militias and special military units to believe that all Tutsi posed a genocidal threat to the existence of Hutu and would enslave Hutu if they ever again became the rulers of Rwanda.

## Genocide Prevention and the Responsibility to Protect

The shock waves emanating from the Rwanda genocide forced world leaders at least to acknowledge in principle that the national sovereignty of offending nations cannot trump the responsibility of those governments to prevent the infliction of mass atrocities on their own people. When governments violate that obligation, the member states of the United Nations have a responsibility to get involved. Such involvement can take the form of, first, offering to help the local government change its ways through technical advice and development aid, and second—if the local government persists in assaulting its own people—initiating armed intervention to protect the civilians at risk. In 2005 the United Nations began to implement the Responsibility to Protect initiative, a framework of principles to guide the international community in preventing mass atrocities.

As in many real-world domains, theory and practice often diverge. Genocide and crimes against humanity are rooted in problems that produce failing states: poverty, poor education, extreme nationalism, lawlessness, dictatorship, and corruption. Implementing the principles of the Responsibility to Protect doctrine burdens intervening state leaders with the necessity of addressing each of those problems over a long period of time. And when those problems prove too intractable and complex to solve easily, the citizens of the intervening nations may lose patience, voting out the leader who initiated the intervention. Arguments based solely on humanitarian principles fail to overcome such concerns. What is needed to persuade political leaders to stop preventable mass atrocities are compelling arguments based on their own national interests.

Preventable mass atrocities threaten the national interests of all states in five specific ways:

1. Mass atrocities create conditions that engender widespread and concrete threats from terrorism, piracy, and other forms of lawlessness on the land and sea;
2. Mass atrocities facilitate the spread of warlordism, whose tentacles block affordable access to vital raw materials produced in the affected country and threaten the prosperity of all nations that depend on the consumption of these resources;
3. Mass atrocities trigger cascades of refugees and internally displaced populations that, combined with climate change and growing international air travel, will accelerate the

worldwide incidence of lethal infectious diseases;

4. Mass atrocities spawn single-interest parties and political agendas that drown out more diverse political discourse in the countries where the atrocities take place and in the countries that host large numbers of refugees. Xenophobia and nationalist backlashes are the predictable consequences of government indifference to mass atrocities elsewhere that could have been prevented through early actions;

5. Mass atrocities foster the spread of national and transnational criminal networks trafficking in drugs, women, arms, contraband, and laundered money.

Alerting elected political representatives to the consequences of mass atrocities should be part of every student movement's agenda in the twenty-first century. Adam Smith, the great political economist and author of *The Wealth of Nations*, put it best when he wrote: "It is not from the benevolence of the butcher, the brewer, or the baker that we expect our dinner, but from their regard to their own interest." Self-interest is a powerful engine for good in the marketplace and can be an equally powerful motive and source of inspiration for state action to prevent genocide and mass persecution. In today's new global village, the lives we save may be our own.

*Frank Chalk*

*Frank Chalk, who has a doctorate from the University of Wisconsin-Madison, is a professor of history and director of the Montreal Institute for Genocide and Human Rights Studies at Concordia University in Montreal, Canada. He is coauthor, with Kurt*

*Jonassohn, of* The History and Sociology of Genocide *(1990); coauthor with General Roméo Dallaire, Kyle Matthews, Carla Barqueiro, and Simon Doyle of* Mobilizing the Will to Intervene: Leadership to Prevent Mass Atrocities *(2010); and associate editor of the three-volume Macmillan Reference USA* Encyclopedia of Genocide and Crimes Against Humanity *(2004). Chalk served as president of the International Association of Genocide Scholars from June 1999 to June 2001. His current research focuses on the use of radio and television broadcasting in the incitement and prevention of genocide, and domestic laws on genocide. For more information on genocide and examples of the experiences of people displaced by genocide and other human rights violations, interested readers can consult the websites of the Montreal Institute for Genocide and Human Rights Studies (http://migs.concordia.ca) and the Montreal Life Stories project (www.lifestoriesmontreal.ca).*

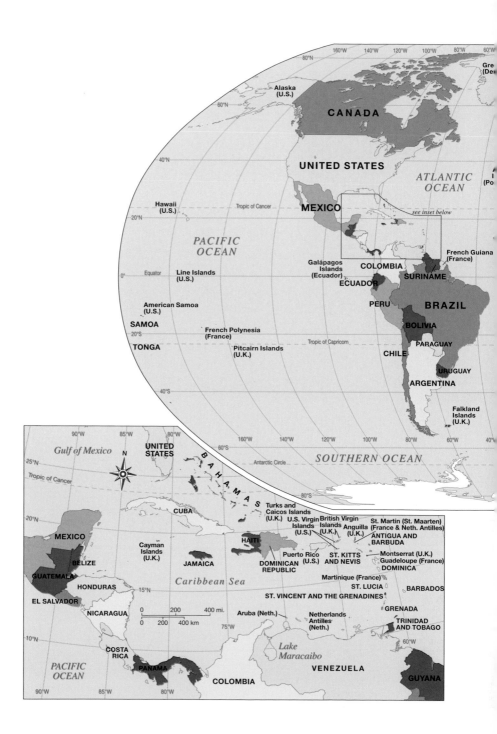

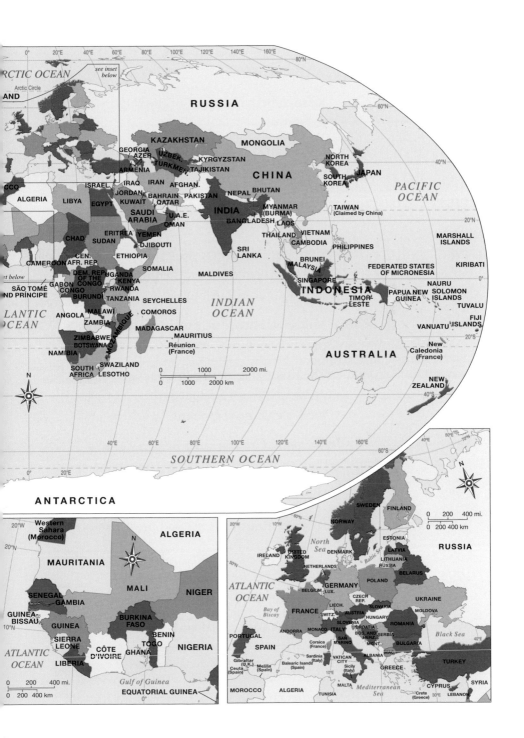

# Chronology

| | |
|---|---|
| **1946** | Kosovo becomes part of the Yugoslav federation. |
| **1974** | Yugoslavia gives Kosovo de facto self-government. |
| **1981** | Separatist rioting in Kosovo is suppressed by Yugoslav troops. |
| **1987** | Slobodan Milosevic addresses Kosovo Serbs and encourages them in their protests against the Albanian majority. |
| **1989** | Milosevic, now the president of Serbia, removes Kosovo's rights to autonomy. |
| **July 1990** | The Kosovo government declares independence from Serbia. Serbia dissolves the Kosovo government. |
| **1991** | Slovenia, Croatia, and Bosnia declare their independence from Yugoslavia. |
| **1992** | War breaks out in Bosnia. |
| **July 1992** | Ibrahim Rugova is elected president of Kosovo. |
| **1994** | NATO launches airstrikes against Bosnian Serbs. |
| **November 21, 1995** | The Dayton Accord ends the war in Bosnia. |
| **1996** | The Kosovo Liberation Army (KLA) begins attacks against Serb authorities in Kosovo. |

| | |
|---|---|
| **March 1998** | Attacks by the KLA escalate in March, prompting a crackdown by Serb forces. |
| **September 1998** | NATO demands that Milosevic cease the crackdown on Kosovo Albanians. He does not. |
| **February 6, 1999** | The Rambouillet peace talks begin in France to resolve the Kosovo conflict. Milosevic refuses to attend. |
| **March 24, 1999** | NATO launches airstrikes against Serbia. |
| **March–June 1999** | Widespread killings and forced expulsions of Kosovo Albanians escalate. |
| **May 27, 1999** | The International War Crimes Tribunal indicts Milosevic for war crimes. |
| **June 20, 1999** | After Milosevic agrees to withdraw troops from Kosovo, the NATO bombing campaign ends. |
| **June–July, 1999** | Kosovo Albanians launch reprisal attacks against Serbs and Roma in Kosovo. |
| **February 2002** | Rugova is elected president of the Kosovo parliament. |
| **March 11, 2006** | Milosevic dies in his prison cell in The Hague. His trial is never completed. |
| **February 2008** | Kosovo declares independence. Many European nations and the United States recognize its independence. Serbia says the declaration is illegal. As of 2012, it still has not recognized Kosovo's independence. |

# CHAPTER 1

# Historical Background on Kosovo

# Chapter Exercises

| STATISTICS | | |
|---|---|---|
| | **Kosovo** | **Serbia** |
| **Total Area** | 10,887 sq mi<br>World ranking: 169 | 77,474 sq mi<br>World ranking: 117 |
| **Population** | 1,825,632<br>World ranking: 148 | 7,210,555<br>World ranking: 98 |
| **Ethnic Groups** | Albanians 92%, other (includes Serb, Bosniak, Gorani, Roma, Turk, Ashkali, Egyptian) 8% | Serb 82.9%, Hungarian 3.9%, Romany (Gypsy) 1.4%, Yugoslav 1.1%, Bosniak 1.8%, Montenegrin 0.9%, other 8% |
| **Religions** | Muslim, Serbian Orthodox, Roman Catholic | Serbian Orthodox 85%, Catholic 5.5%, Protestant 1.1%, Muslim 3.2%, unspecified 2.6%, other, unknown or atheist, 2.6% |
| **Literacy** (total population) | 91.9% | 96.4% |
| **GDP** | $11.97 billion<br>World ranking: 144<br>GDP per capita: $6,600 | $80.1 billion<br>World ranking: 78<br>GDP per capita: $10,900 |

Source: *The World Factbook*. Washington, DC: Central Intelligence Agency, 2012. www.cia.gov.

## 1. Analyzing Statistics: Kosovo and Serbia

**Question 1:** In Kosovo, which is the largest ethnic group? Which group initially experienced ethnic cleansing and oppression in the first part of the Kosovo crisis? How was this possible? (Consider the population figures for Serbia as well.)

**Question 2:** GDP is the total economic output of a country in a year; GDP per capita is the total economic output divided by the population of the country in the same year. Based on the figures, is Serbia's GDP greater than Kosovo's just because Serbia is larger than Kosovo? Or are the people of Kosovo actually individually poorer than the people of Serbia? How might this have affected the ethnic struggle in Kosovo?

**Question 3:** The figures above show that Serbs make up only a small percentage of the people in Kosovo, and ethnic Albanians make up an even smaller percentage of people in Serbia. These figures are taken from the period after the Kosovo crisis ended. Before the crisis, do you think the number of Serbs in Kosovo, and of ethnic Albanians in Serbia, was higher or lower? How and why did the crisis change the population distribution?

## 2. Writing Prompt

Imagine you are a reporter in a refugee camp in Albania talking to refugees that have fled from Serb violence in Kosovo. Report on the experiences of the refugees. Begin the article with a strong title that will captivate the audience. Give details to explain the event and answer who, what, when, where, and why.

## 3. Group Activity

Imagine your class can go back in time to the period just before NATO decided to bomb Serbia. Get together in small groups and develop speeches to make to NATO either recommending that bombing commence or recommending not bombing Serbia. Use your knowledge of the outcome of the bombings and of the fate of Kosovo and Serbia to make your case.

# Overview of Kosovo and Serbia

*Kathleen Z. Young*

*In the following viewpoint, Western Washington University an-thropology professor Kathleen Z. Young discusses the history of Albanians and Serbians in Kosovo. She points out that the two groups share animosities going back more than six hundred years. The most recent round of conflicts occurred following the breakup of Yugoslavia in the early 1990s, a time when Kosovo was under Serbia control and had little autonomy. By the mid-1990s a re-sistance group, the Kosovo Liberation Army, began agitating for independence; Serbia, under the leadership of Slobodan Milosevic, refused and sent troops into Kosovo, claiming to represent the in-terests of ethnic Serbs in Kosovo. In 1999 NATO (North Atlantic Treaty Organization) launched a bombing campaign against Serbia in an attempt to end what was seen as a military occupa-tion of Kosovo by Serbia; the bombings were followed by atroci-ties committed by Serbs against Albanians, forcing eight hundred thousand to flee the country, according to Young. NATO troops es-calated the bombing; soon after, Serb troops were withdrawn from Kosovo. At that point Albanians returned and unleashed a wave of terror against Serbs. Though the conflict ended in 1999, violence broke out again in 2004. Young explains that the ethnic tensions and bitterness still linger.*

Kosovo was ineluctably tied to Serbia at the Battle of Kosovo Polje in 1389, wherein the victorious Muslim Turks left the dead for blackbirds to scavenge, according to Serbian folklore. Kosovo was then etched in Serbian ethno-religious consciousness as a place of Serbian torment and sacrifice, ushering in five hundred years of Turkish domination. The Battle of Kosovo marked the end of the Serbian empire. The Turks conquered Albania by 1468, but although most Albanians converted to Islam, they maintained their separate ethnic identity.

## Serbs vs. Albanians

Ottoman [that is, Turkish] rule was ending by 1878. Serbia, Montenegro, Greece, and Bulgaria amassed troops and finally succeeded in driving out the Ottoman forces in the Balkan Wars (1912–1913). The geographical extent of Albania was reduced at the behest of France and Russia, leaving more than half of the total Albanian population outside the borders of the diminished state, and placing the area of Kosovo within Serbia. The Serbian victors massacred entire Albanian villages, looting and burning anything that remained. European press reports estimated that Serbs killed 25,000 Albanians.

From the end of the Balkan Wars to World War II, Albanians lived under Serb domination. Their language was suppressed, their land confiscated, and their mosques were turned into stables, all part of an overt Serb policy designed to pressure Muslim Albanians to leave Kosovo. The cycle of revanchism (revenge-based conflict) continued when a part of Kosovo was united with Albania by Italian fascists during World War II and Albanian Nazi collaborators expelled an estimated forty thousand Serbs.

A postwar Constitution, adopted in 1946, defined Yugoslavia as a federal state of six sovereign republics. Kosovo was granted autonomy, allowing it to have representatives in the federal legislature yet keeping its internal affairs under Serbian control. In 1948, Yugoslavia broke away from [Joseph] Stalin's [Communist] Russia, a move that pitted the Albanian Kosovars against the

## The Disintegration of Yugoslavia

Following the death of [Yugoslavian] President Josip Broz Tito in 1980, the gradual disintegration of communist Yugoslavia created a power vacuum that allowed extreme nationalist movements to undermine the country's stability and social cohesion. In Kosovo, the ethnic Albanian Muslim majority and the ethnic Serbian orthodox Christian minority had engaged in nationalist political struggles throughout the 1970s and 1980s. These developments facilitated the rise of Slobodan Milosevic's virulently nationalist Socialist Party of Serbia and allowed Milosevic to assume the presidency of Serbia in 1989. In the same year, Milosevic annulled Kosovo's provincial autonomy in language and education, and asserted Serbian political and cultural hegemony from Belgrade. Political divisions deepened after the collapse of the Yugoslav Communist Party in 1990 and the abrogation of the federation's one-party system. As head of the Serbian Socialist Party, Milosevic continued to rally nationalist sentiment using his control of the state media, through which he promoted the idea of a "Greater Serbia" that would incorporate the ethnic Serbian regions of other Yugoslav republics.

In July 1990, Kosovo's ethnic Albanian political leaders declared independence. Serbian authorities countered this unconstitutional development with intensified repression in Kosovo, including the closing of Albanian-language newspapers, the renaming of Albanian streets in Serbian, and the introduction of compulsory Serbian curricula in Kosovar Albanian-majority educational institutions.

*Frank Chalk, Kyle Matthews, and Carla Barqueiro,* Mobilizing the Will to Intervene: Leadership to Prevent Mass Atrocities. *Quebec, Canada: McGill-Queen's University Press, 2010, pp. 38–39.*

country of Albania, which was staunchly pro-Russian. Yugoslav and Albanian border guards clashed along the Albanian border, and the Yugoslav secret police intensified its persecution of ethnic Albanians in Kosovo. As Serbs persecuted Albanian-Kosovars, the Kosovars harassed Serbs in turn.

Demographic studies from 1979 show that Albanian Kosovars had the highest population growth rate in Europe, especially in rural areas. Increasing numbers of young ethnic Albanians were under the age of 25 and unemployed, fueling dissent. When the President of Yugoslavia, Croat-born Marshal [Josip Broz] Tito, allowed an Albanian-language university to be established in Kosovo, it became the center of Albanian national identity. Following Tito's death in 1980, students demonstrated for better living conditions in 1981, inspiring construction and factory workers to take to the streets in protest throughout Kosovo.

Retribution was immediate and harsh. The Yugoslav army was sent to Kosovo, killing Albanians and arresting people for "verbal crimes," for which substantial prison sentences were imposed. The press, local governments, and schools were purged of the Albanians who held such jobs (most such employees were Serbs). At the same time, approximately 30,000 Serbs left Kosovo (according to Yugoslav government estimates), ostensibly because of Albanian retaliation. Critics, however, have suggested that the Serbs left for economic reasons. The Yugoslav government economic policy toward Kosovo was one of resource extraction. Wealth, in the form of minerals, was siphoned out of Kosovo for the benefit of the other republics, with very little ever coming back to the impoverished area.

## The Breakup of Yugoslavia

In the mid-1980s Serb-Kosovars complained to the Yugoslav government that the escalating ethnic Albanian birthrate constituted a willful plot against the Serbs. Ethnic Albanian women stopped going to government-run hospitals to have babies, fearing that Serb doctors would kill their babies to reduce the birthrate. In 1987, Slobodan Milosevic attended a meeting in Kosovo during which a raucous crowd of Serbs tried to push their way in. Milosevic commanded the police to let "his" Serbs through, establishing himself as the savior of Serbs outside the borders of Serbia. Critics allege that the event was arranged in advance. After Milosevic was elected President of Serbia in 1990; Albanian police officers in Kosovo were suspended from their jobs and replaced with 2,500 Serb policemen imported from Belgrade.

In the spring of 1990, thousands of Albanian schoolchildren became sick and were hospitalized, and it was rumored that Serbs had poisoned them. When Albanian parents attacked Serb property in response, Milosevic immediately transferred another 25,000 police to the area. Serb police were allowed to keep Albanians in jail for three days without charges, and to imprison anyone for up to two months if they had been charged with insulting the "patriotic feelings" of Serbs. The conflict in Kosovo and the Serb annexation of the province in 1987 led to concerns in the other republics that Serbia was intending to transform Yugoslavia into "Greater Serbia." However, the pattern of revanchism in response to the mounting human rights abuses was broken when Albanians turned to passive resistance, following the model of non-violence espoused by Mahatma Gandhi.

The Serb war against Bosnia[1] from 1992 to 1995 worsened the situation for Albanians in Kosovo. This time, Albanians suffered from the anti-Muslim fervor of Serbs and the hardships resulting from the economic sanctions imposed by the United Nations in response to the war. The Bosnian war ended with the negotiation of the Dayton Accords in 1995, but Kosovo was left out of the discussion. Disappointed Kosovars watched Western diplomats congratulate Milosevic on his peacemaking efforts. Albanian Kosovars continued their practice of passive resistance until 1997, when the country of Albania collapsed into chaos and Kosovo was flooded with weapons from across the border. The ethnic majority, Albanian Kosovars, now had access to weapons, a serious concern for the Serbs. Suspected members of the newly formed Kosovo Liberation Army were arrested and charged with "hostile association," a charge that was never denied.

## War and NATO

A Serb policeman was murdered in 1998, prompting a police attack on a village in which one hundred Albanians were killed. Further massacres of Albanians continued to fuel the mobilization of the Kosovo Liberation Army. As Muslim refugees streamed into Albania, Serbs lined the borders with landmines. An estimated 270,000 Albanians fled to the hills of Kosovo. In the fall of 1998, NATO [North Atlantic Treaty Organization] authorized air strikes against Serb military targets and Milosevic agreed to withdraw his troops. By the winter of 1998, however, the United States was proclaiming that Serbs were committing "crimes against humanity" in Kosovo.

Negotiations to offset the looming humanitarian disaster and end the alleged Serb crimes were fashioned in Rambouillet, France, in early 1999. The peace plan proposed by the United Nations was rejected by both Serbs and Albanian Kosovars. The political blueprint called for NATO troops to be placed in Kosovo to oversee peace and protect the combatants from each other, but Serbia rejected the presence of foreign troops on its soil. A United Nations force, similar to the peacekeepers in Bosnia, might have been accepted, but the West insisted on a NATO force. The ostensible reason for this insistence was that the West wanted to avoid a replay situation that occurred in Bosnia. There, the peacekeepers were forced to stand by idly and watch Bosnian women and children be killed. For their part, the Kosovo Liberation Army (KLA) refused to comply with the Rambouillet mandate that they disarm. There had been too many instances in Bosnia, they argued, where Muslims disarmed and put themselves under the protection of the United Nations, only to be murdered by Serbs. This had occurred in Srebenica in 1995, when approximately seven thousand boys and old men were murdered by Serbs while in a United Nations designated safe-haven.

With the negotiations stalled, Serbia sent 40,000 troops to the border of Kosovo, exploiting the break in diplomacy to further what appeared to be preparations for an all-out occupation of Kosovo. Fearing a blood bath, knowing the far superior military strength of the Serb army, and with knowledge of the atrocities committed in Bosnia, the Albanians agreed to the stipulations of the Rambouillet treaty. Hundreds of thousands of ethnic Albanians were hiding in the winter hills, thousands more were displaced, and over 2,000 civilians had been killed. The KLA signed the treaty. NATO threatened Serbia with bombing if it refused to sign, but NATO had made such threats before, and the powers in Belgrade had no reason to believe action would be taken against them this time. Despite the NATO rhetoric, they refused.

NATO began bombing strategic targets in Kosovo on March 24, 1999, in response to Serbia's "Operation Horseshoe" [the name of the anti-Albanian offensive]. Fanning out into the region in a pattern that took on the shape of a horseshoe, Serb soldiers went village-to-village, killing and burning, forcing those who could to run for their lives. To many, it looked as if the NATO bombings caused the extraordinary events that followed. Within three days of the bombing, 25,000 Albanian Kosovars were fleeing in terror. Within weeks 800,000 were fleeing. Serbian border guards took their identification papers and money, destroying any proof they ever existed.

## Atrocities

Televised satellite technology yielded pictures of mass graves. Serbs then moved the remains and burned their victims, leaving the victims' families with no way of knowing what had happened to their missing relatives. A common means of disposal was to throw bodies into a well or water supply, rendering the water undrinkable. Cultural monuments and Islamic religious sites were destroyed. Reports estimated that up to 20,000 rapes and sexual assaults were committed against Albanian women.

*An Albanian child looks at a memorial wall of people missing and presumed dead after the 1999 war in Kosovo. The fate of many missing Albanians remained unknown for many years after the war.* © Chris Hondros/Getty Images News/Getty Images.

Albanian residents in Mitrovica were expelled, their houses and mosques burned, and women were sexually assaulted during attacks beginning on March 25, 1999. Albanians in other areas, most notably Pristina, were also expelled or killed, and women here, too, were sexually assaulted.

By May 20, 1999, one-third of the Albanian population had been expelled from Kosovo. The refugee crisis overwhelmed Macedonia and Albania, threatening to undermine the weak economies of both countries and flood the rest of Europe with refugees and asylum seekers from Kosovo. The International Criminal Tribunal for the Former Yugoslavia, convened to prosecute war crimes in Bosnia, indicted Milosevic for crimes against humanity in Kosovo on May 27, 1999, and NATO escalated its air strikes. With questionable legality, NATO bombed the capital of Serbia, Belgrade, accidentally including in its targets a maternity hospital and the Chinese embassy. On June 2, 1999, Milosevic capitulated to the terms of NATO, and within ten days, Serb troops began pulling out of Kosovo. Between mid-June, when the NATO troops were deployed, and mid-August, 1999, more than 755,000 Kosovars returned to Kosovo.

The situation was reversed for the Serbs. There were an estimated 20,000 Serbs in Pristina, Kosovo, before the NATO bombing. By mid-August, the United Nations High Commission of Refugees reported only 2,000 Serbs left in the capital city, and increasingly violent attacks on the Serb population by Albanian Kosovars were on the rise. Albanian Kosovars used the same tactics that Serbs had used against them, forcing Serbs to sign over their property and possessions and leave. Nearly 200,000 Serb refugees from Kosovo fled into Serbia and Montenegro as the Albanian-Kosovars returned. Again, the departure was abrupt and fearful. The United Nations and NATO asserted their presence in the area, providing the appearance of protection for the now targeted Serbs. Nonetheless, tensions between ethnic Serbs and Albanians erupted into violent conflict again in Kosovo in March 2004. Albanian violence against Serbs was especially pronounced in areas where the International Criminal Tribunal for the Former Yugoslavia had documented atrocities committed against Albanians, especially around the areas of Mitrovica and Pristina, Kosovo. The violence in March 2004 left nineteen dead. Serbian Orthodox monasteries were demolished, and Serb houses and property were burned and destroyed. Intense debate regarding the partition of Kosovo from Serbia and Serbs from Albanian Kosovars was given new immediacy, but all sides were entrenched in their oppositional positions.

The trial of Milosevic by the International Criminal Tribunal for the Former Yugoslavia commenced on October 29, 2001, in which he was charged with genocide, crimes against humanity, murder, and persecution (including command responsibility for the sexual assaults on Kosovo Albanian women and the wanton destruction of religious sites) in Kosovo. The prosecution rested its case in February 2004, with the United Nations allowing the defense, judgment, and appeals processes to extend through 2010. The legacy of ethnic cleansing touched everyone throughout the former Yugoslavia. Thousands of Roma (Gypsy) who lived in Kosovo and the surrounding areas remained homeless and have been overlooked by the judicial process. For the Kosovars—both Albanian and Serb—history and experience have provided no solid template for establishing peace.

## Note

1. Bosnia declared independence from Serbia in 1991. Ethnic Serbs and Croats in Bosnia rejected independence, which prompted a civil war.

# The Kosovo Liberation Army Rises as a Force in Kosovo

*Henry H. Perritt Jr.*

*Henry H. Perritt Jr. is a professor of law and former dean at the Chicago-Kent College of Law. In the following viewpoint, he describes the rise of the Kosovo Liberation Army (KLA) and its ultimate success in establishing an independent Kosovo. He discusses the longstanding tensions between Albanians and Serbs that led to the rise of the KLA. He argues that the KLA was successful as an insurgency for several reasons: though Muslim, the KLA did not associate with international Islamic fundamentalist groups; the KLA did not use terror against civilians; and the KLA successfully cultivated relations with the Albanian community. For these reasons, he says, the KLA managed to successfully appeal for international support against Serbia.*

The Kosovo Liberation Army (KLA) was one of the most successful insurgencies of the post-cold war period, although it engaged in a relatively short period of widespread armed conflict. It illustrated the twentieth-century apogee of "Fourth Generation War" or "4GW," a term that signifies the integration

Henry H. Perritt Jr., *Kosovo Liberation Army: The Inside Story of an Insurgency*. Champaign: University of Illinois Press, 2008, pp. 2–9. Copyright © 2008 by University of Illinois Press. All rights reserved. Reproduced by permission.

of political and military aspects of warfare. Guerrilla attacks are a means not only of holding territory or destroying foreign forces, but of moving the hearts and minds of those among whom the guerrillas operate, within the populations of foreign states whose policies could make or break the resistance, and of the fighters themselves.

## Insurgency Without Terrorism

In many respects, the development of the KLA followed the pattern of other insurgencies around the world. It flourished only when it had broad popular support, while its activities helped to build that support. It recruited fighters and less-active supporters in proportion to growing oppression by the regime it opposed, repression stimulated by KLA tactics. Continued existence of the KLA depended on the execution of a sophisticated public relations strategy aimed not only at the local population but also at the international community. It depended on financial support from outside, and on a reliable flow of appropriate arms.

Unlike other insurgencies, however, the KLA made relatively little use of terrorist attacks on civilian targets. It also won relatively few battles against opposing military forces. Its evolution into a full-fledged guerrilla force engaged in a war of attrition was interrupted by its success in the political arena. Although the KLA insurgency took place in a region where the population was predominantly Muslim, it rebuffed offers of aid from Islamic fundamentalists. . . .

The KLA was an exemplar of 4GW concepts, and its story reinforces well-understood precepts about insurgency developed in the late twentieth and early twenty-first centuries. Insurgencies flourish only when they have support from the civilian population in which they operate; they are most often fueled by nationalism—a product of the nineteenth century; and they are most successful when they oppose regimes that can be characterized as foreign occupiers. They can effectively oppose military forces that are vastly superior in numerical, technological, and organizational terms, because they rely on hit-and-run ambushes, and hide among a local population where the opposing forces, often ethnically and linguistically foreign, cannot identify them. Insurgencies are difficult to stamp out once they reach a critical mass of fighters and popular support. Guerrillas have a politico-military advantage; they are almost impossible to defend against. Trying to annihilate them usually builds popular support for them. "Massacres" by the military and police forces of a regime often fuel an explosion of recruits for an insurgency. Successful insurgencies usually rely on external financial support and arms supplies. They develop more quickly when they have safe areas in which to train, to resupply, to reorganize, and to rest. Passionate young people without much training or experience can lead insurgencies successfully.

Despite these reasons for classifying it as a model insurgency, the quick success of the Kosovo Liberation Army owed predominantly to an unusual configuration of geopolitical and popular phenomena. The stars, it seemed, aligned just as the KLA reached the point at which it could operate effectively all over Kosovo, and as it had achieved a sophisticated understanding of how to use armed force to shape international public opinion. Crucial to the success of the KLA was its prowess in presenting its case to the outside world. Looking forward, however, replicating KLA strategies in other insurgencies would have a less dramatic effect. The international community was especially receptive in 1998 and 1999 to the possibility of a human rights intervention in Kosovo because of the bloodshed in Bosnia[1] and the absence of strategic threats sufficient to refocus major-power attention on other places. Further, the KLA understood diaspora power. Efforts at raising money and recruiting soldiers from the Albanian Diaspora were energetic, and mobilization of Diaspora voices in domestic political forums was strong. Eventually the U.S. Congress, the British Parliament, and the German Bundestag listened.

The KLA experience also shows that not every nominally Muslim population will buy into Islamic fundamentalism and align itself with [international terrorist organization] Al-Qaeda when it is pursuing primarily nationalist goals. Far more than religion motivated the KLA. Indeed, religion was largely irrelevant; a number of the KLA's most enthusiastic fighters and fund raisers were Catholic rather than Muslim. Islam was essentially irrelevant as a driver of the insurgency, and Muslim religious affiliation did not interfere with a passionate pro-American stance after the conflict ended. Moreover, the KLA listened when the United States said, through the CIA, "Don't get involved with Islamic extremists." What mattered was not religious reverence but political humiliation. In Kosovo, recruitment was made easier—indeed made possible in the first place—by Serb policies under Slobodan Milosevic that were disdainful of values held by the Albanian community. . . .

## The Albanians in Kosovo

The background of the Kosovo conflict can be confusing. The first potential source of confusion is that the majority population in Kosovo is ethnic Albanian, but there also exists a separate state called "Albania." The second potential source of confusion is Kosovo's multilayered political and legal relationship with Yugoslavia. Those preliminary matters should be sorted out. Kosovo is a small, diamond-shaped patch of land that is about three-quarters the size of the Chicago metropolitan area. At the outbreak of the KLA insurgency, it was part of Serbia, which in turn was the dominant republic within Yugoslavia. Albanians are a distinct ethnic group concentrated in the southwestern part of the Balkans in southeastern Europe. Some three and one-half million Albanians live in the Republic of Albania, about two million in Kosovo, a half million in the northern and western parts of Macedonia, and a hundred thousand or so in Montenegro. Defined more by language, history, and culture than by race or religion, Albanians proudly trace their history to the Illyrian people, who flourished along the Balkan Peninsula before the Roman Empire subdued and integrated them.

*Kosovo Liberation Army soldiers monitor Serb forces from the frontline trenches in the Podujevo region of Kosovo in February 1999.* © Tyler Hicks/Getty Images News/Getty Images.

The antecedents of Albanian discontent with foreign domination in Kosovo stretch back for centuries. In every generation, Albanians living in the southwest Balkans engaged in armed resistance or mass demonstrations, or both, seeking to displace Turkish or Slavic regimes that denied their national aspirations. Each time, the regime crushed the resistance, bought it off with modest concessions, or both. Fragmented politically, and isolated from the rest of the world because of rugged geography, the Albanian region was regularly divided by a succession of empires. The Ottoman Empire in particular divided the Albanian territories into separate *pashalets* (imperial administrative units). The modern state of Albania was assembled and granted recognition as an independent state at the end of the First Balkan War in 1912–13 in the Treaties of London and Bucharest. Its borders were confirmed in the "Paris Peace Conference" following World War I, which redrew the map of Europe after the collapse of the Ottoman and Austro-Hungarian Empires. Pleas by the Albanian people for incorporation into an enlarged state of Albania fell on deaf ears. Meanwhile, the region that came to be known as Yugoslavia was being acknowledged as a state by the Paris Conference diplomats as they mostly formalized realities on the ground. Croatia, Serbia, Slovenia, Macedonia, Bosnia, Montenegro, and Kosovo were all glued together into a "Kingdom of Serbs, Slovenes and Croats." This kingdom was not a product of nationalism but rather of pragmatism. It tottered through the interwar period, its politics dominated by assassinations and ethnically based intrigue. During World War II, the Balkan region was a major battlefield. Italy set up an administrative and political unit encompassing most of the Albanian population early in the war, and comprising the territories of the state of Albania and significant parts of Serbia, Kosovo, Macedonia, and a sliver of Montenegro.

The war ended for most of Europe in June 1945 but went on in the Balkans for another three years until the Communist forces, led by Josip Broz (Tito) and Enver Hoxha, came out on top. Tito consolidated his territories into a state called "Yugoslavia," "the union of the southern Slavs," while Hoxha kept the state of Albania. Tito divided Yugoslavia into six separate republics: Slovenia, Croatia, Bosnia, Serbia, Montenegro, and Macedonia. Serbia, by far the largest, was further divided into three parts: a central region and two provinces. These two provinces were geographically and ethnically distinct from each other and from the central region. Vojvodina, the northern and larger province, was made up of a mixture of Serbs, Hungarians, and other ethnic groups while Kosovo, to the south, was populated mostly by ethnic Albanians but had a significant Serb minority. As a province within a republic, Kosovo had less autonomy than if it had been a republic on its own.

The Kosovar Albanians, already feeling betrayed by Kosovo's incorporation into Serbia rather than Albania after the collapse of the Ottoman Empire, had tasted the flavor of a unified Albanian "state" during the wartime Italian occupation. Now they had been betrayed again, despite Tito's promise toward the end of the war that they could decide through a referendum whether they wanted to be part of Albania or Yugoslavia. The very name "Yugoslavia" caused Kosovar Albanians to bristle. As noted above, "Yugoslavia" translates roughly as "union of the southern Slavs." The dominant populations of the six Yugoslav republics *were* Slavs—Slovenes, Croats, most Macedonians, Bosniaks, and Serbs, all of whom could point to Slavic ancestors and spoke Slavic languages at home. Albanians were not Slavs, and those in Kosovo saw no reason they should be forced to be part of Yugoslavia rather than of the independent state of Albania next door. Moreover, they spoke Albanian—a completely different language from the Serbo-Croatian used in most of the rest of Yugoslavia.

The KLA story can be told chronologically or thematically. The following paragraphs provide a chronological summary. . . . Five time periods bracket the major developments.

## 1945–1985: Restless Nationalism Erupts Sporadically

Yugoslav strongman Marshal Tito alternated between placating Albanian nationalism by allowing greater autonomy and ruthlessly insisting on assimilation of all ethnic groups into a new "Yugoslav" culture. The Kosovar Albanian experience inside Yugoslavia was therefore tumultuous. As World War II concluded, some thirty thousand Yugoslav Partisan troops suppressed a revolt by the same young Albanian fighters who had helped the Partisans drive Axis forces from Kosovo. In February 1945, Tito declared martial law in Kosovo. Thereafter, Serb authorities prohibited the display of Albanian flags and other nationalist symbols, and treated teaching of Albanian history and literature as a deviation from Communist doctrine. Serbs held all of the main Communist Party and government offices in Kosovo. Hoxha's alignment with [Russian dictator Joseph] Stalin against Tito only fueled Serb suspicions that Albanians in Kosovo were a security threat. From 1947 to his downfall in 1966, Serbian Minister of the Interior Aleksandar Rankovic oversaw ruthless Serb security forces in Kosovo, confiscated Albanian weapons, and pressed Albanians to emigrate. Both Rankovic's removal from office in 1966 and Tito's 1968 offer of more opportunities to Kosovar Albanians gave breathing space at last to Albanian nationalism, which, paradoxically, led to widespread riots in 1968 supporting incorporation of Kosovo and Albanian areas of Macedonia either into Albania or into a new Albanian republic in Yugoslavia. Tito responded with half a loaf: establishment of an Albanian-language university in Prishtina in 1969 and greater political autonomy to Kosovars under a new constitution adopted in 1974. Things were calm on the surface, but Kosovo continued to slip behind the rest of Yugoslavia economically, and Serb-Albanian tensions grew as Kosovar Albanians demanded greater political opportunity and Kosovar Serbs resisted it.

In 1981, a few months after Tito's death, massive demonstrations started at the University of Prishtina and rapidly spread throughout Kosovo. Order was restored, but scores of Albanians were killed and thousands more were arrested, often for little more than passing out literature. Others, predominantly young men who managed to avoid arrest, fled mostly to Switzerland or Germany to escape repression and seek better lives. As the numbers of exiles grew throughout the 1980s, leaders of several clandestine organizations worked to reawaken and intensify their sense of Albanian nationalism.

## 1985–1993: Dreams and Plans for a Revolution

The core of these "Planners in Exile"—the LPRK (Popular League for the Republic of Kosovo), which later became the LPK (Popular League for Kosovo)—was in place in Switzerland, Germany, and Albania by 1985. Tiny and obscure, LPRK began making contact with militants inside Kosovo, the "Defenders at Home." It also

tried to learn how to organize a guerrilla insurgency by study-
ing the experiences in Ireland, Vietnam, Algeria, and the Basque
region of Spain; learning where and from whom to get arms;
and crafting a fund-raising network. Meanwhile, the iron curtain was raised[2] and Yugoslavia struggled with political plural-
ism. The Albanian political elite in Kosovo and Serb party boss
Slobodan Milosevic were on a collision course. After Milosevic
consolidated his power in Serbia, he revoked Kosovo's political
autonomy. The Kosovar Albanian elite formed its own political
party, the Democratic League of Kosovo (LDK), declared independence, and established in Germany a "Government in Exile."
For a time, some of these "Peaceful Path Institutionalists" tried
to work with the Planners in Exile and the Defenders at Home.
They organized training camps in Albania for would-be Albanian
guerrilla fighters, but the training program was infiltrated by the
Serb secret police in 1993, and almost everyone was arrested or
dispersed back into exile before they could do anything.

## 1993–1996: The Intelligence War

The LPRK changed its name and organized the Kosovo Liberation
Army. From 1993 to 1996, the KLA worked to recover from the
1993 arrests and to consolidate recruitment, fund raising, and
logistics structures for war. It sent agents on missions around
Kosovo to identify and recruit people to replace those who had
been arrested. It was nearly invisible inside Kosovo, among the
Diaspora, and to the international community. This silent period
from 1993 to 1996 was the period during which the KLA fought
and won an "intelligence war." Winning the intelligence war
meant two things. First, it meant preventing penetration of the
KLA. Second, it meant eliminating or intimidating individuals
who were formally or informally part of the Serb secret police.

## 1996–1998: The KLA's War for Popular Opinion

The 1995 signing of the Dayton Accords [peace agreement] dis-
credited the Peaceful Path Institutionalists. Although Kosovar

Albanians had waited to be rescued from Milosevic by the international community rather than fighting his regime as did the Croats and Bosnians, the international community concentrated its attention on stopping the war in Bosnia and ignored Kosovo. Support for the KLA grew inside Kosovo, and it gradually accelerated the pace of its attacks on police stations and convoys and on collaborators. The government of the state of Albania collapsed in the spring of 1997, clearing the way for substantial shipments of arms. Milosevic's forces, now freed from the wars in Croatia and Bosnia, began to turn their attention to Kosovo, intending to stamp out the emerging insurgency.

## 1998: A Shooting War

Milosevic's aggressive attempt to annihilate the KLA backfired. A siege on the home of KLA leader Adem Jashari, one of several launched on leading families of the Defenders at Home in the spring of 1998, resulted in the deaths of nearly sixty individuals, including women, the elderly, and young children, as well as Jashari himself. Instead of squelching the insurgency, the attack galvanized Kosovo and horrified the rest of the world. Leaders of the Planners in Exile returned to Kosovo. Overwhelmed with volunteers and struggling to arm them through the supply chain now functioning through the recently collapsed state of Albania, the KLA made use of its newfound riches by broadening its attacks and declaring itself to be an "army" rather than a mere guerrilla movement. As the scale of military conflict escalated, and as hundreds of thousands of Kosovar Albanian refugees overwhelmed the capacity of neighboring Albania and Macedonia to deal with them, the international community no longer could sit back, smug with the success of the Dayton Accords. Frantic diplomacy followed, but was only frustrated by Milosevic's intransigent insistence on his sovereign prerogatives to deal with internal "terrorism" in his own way, by international reluctance to legitimate the KLA by negotiating with it, and then by the difficulty that emerged in figuring out *how* to deal with it. A cease fire in October 1998 permitted the KLA to recover from the Serb onslaught of the late summer and fall, and then renewed fighting in late December and early 1999 produced one last diplomatic effort in Rambouillet, France, in February and March 1999. When Milosevic would not budge, NATO began a campaign of aerial bombardment that ultimately drove Serb forces from Kosovo in June 1999. On or about June 12 (there is some dispute about the date and circumstances of the KLA's entry) the KLA marched into the capital city of Prishtina in uniformed military columns, with flags flying and the Kosovar civilian population throwing flowers at them. Then the KLA disbanded, with some of its soldiers becoming part of the new Kosovo Police Service and others becoming members of a mostly unarmed Kosovo Protection Corps, and some of its leadership beginning to organize new political parties.

## Notes

1. Bosnia, a former Yugoslav republic, was the site of war and atrocities from 1992–1995.
2. Raising the iron curtain refers to the Communist Soviet Union allowing independence in the states it had controlled in Eastern Europe.

# Ethnic Cleansing Took Place in Kosovo

*US Department of State*

*The US Department of State is charged with overseeing US foreign relations. In the following viewpoint, the Department of State documents the atrocities committed against Albanians in the Kosovo War. The authors assert that, based on evidence from mass graves and other reports, around ten thousand Kosovar Albanians were killed by Serb forces. In addition, Serbs undertook a campaign of ethnic cleansing that included forcible displacement of ethnic Albanians, burning of homes, mass rape, and other atrocities. The report concludes that a million Albanians were forced out of the province by Serb action, and 1.5 million, or around 90 percent of the Albanian population in the province, were expelled from their homes.*

The atrocities against Kosovar Albanians documented in this report occurred primarily between March and late June, 1999. . . .

A central question is the number of Kosovar Albanian victims of Serbian forces in Kosovo. Many bodies were found when KFOR [the NATO-led peacekeeping force in Kosovo]

"Ethnic Cleansing in Kosovo: An Accounting," US Department of State, December 1999. www.state.gov.

**REFUGEE MIGRATION DESTINATIONS TO ESCAPE SERBIAN FORCES DURING THE KOSOVO CONFLICT**

Taken from: CNN.com, "Desperate Refugees Flee Kosovo, Accuse Serbs of Atrocities," March 30, 1999. http://edition.cnn.com/WORLD/europe/9903/29/refugees.04.

and the ICTY [International Criminal Tribunal for the former Yugoslavia] entered Kosovo in June 1999. The evidence is also now clear that Serbian forces conducted a systematic campaign to burn or destroy bodies, or to bury the bodies, then rebury them to conceal evidence of Serbian crimes. On June 4, at the end of the conflict, the Department of State issued the last of a series of weekly ethnic cleansing reports . . . concluding that at least 6,000 Kosovar Albanians were victims of mass murder, with an unknown number of victims of individual killings, and an unknown number of bodies burned or destroyed by Serbian forces throughout the conflict.

## Murder and Forcible Expulsion

On November 10, 1999, ICTY Chief Prosecutor Carla Del Ponte told the U.N. Security Council that her office had received reports of more than 11,000 killed in 529 reported mass grave and killing sites in Kosovo. The Prosecutor said her office had exhumed 2,108 bodies from 195 of the 529 known mass graves. This would imply about 6,000 bodies in mass graves in Kosovo if the 334 mass graves not examined thus far contain the same average number of victims. To this total must be added three important categories of victims: (1) those buried in mass graves whose locations are unknown, (2) what the ICTY reports is a significant number of sites where the precise number of bodies cannot be counted, and (3) victims whose bodies were burned or destroyed by Serbian forces. Press accounts and eyewitness accounts provide credible details of a program of destruction of evidence by Serbian forces throughout Kosovo and even in Serbia proper. The number of victims whose bodies have been burned or destroyed may never be known, but enough evidence has emerged to conclude that probably around 10,000 Kosovar Albanians were killed by Serbian forces.

Death represents only one facet of Serbian actions in Kosovo. Over 1.5 million Kosovar Albanians—at least 90 percent of the estimated 1998 Kosovar Albanian population of Kosovo—were forcibly expelled from their homes. Tens of thousands of homes in at least 1,200 cities, towns, and villages have been damaged or destroyed. During the conflict, Serbian forces and paramilitaries implemented a systematic campaign to ethnically cleanse Kosovo—aspects of this campaign include the following:

- *Forcible Displacement of Kosovar Albanian Civilians:* Serbian authorities conducted a campaign of forced population movement. In contrast to actions taken during 1998, Yugoslav Army units and armed civilians joined the police in systematically expelling Kosovar Albanians at gunpoint from both villages and larger towns in Kosovo.

- *Looting of Homes and Businesses:* There are numerous reports of Serbian forces robbing residents before burning their homes. Another round of robbery occurred as Serbian forces stole from fleeing Kosovars as they crossed the border to Montenegro, Albania, or Macedonia.

- *Widespread Burning of Homes:* Over 1,200 residential areas were at least partially burned after late March, 1999. Kosovar Albanians have reported that over 500 villages were burned after March, 1999.

- *Use of Human Shields:* Refugees claim that Serbian forces used Kosovar Albanians to escort military convoys and shield facilities throughout the province. Other reporting indicates that Serbian forces intentionally positioned ethnic Albanians at sites they believed were targets for NATO airstrikes.

- *Detentions:* Serbian forces systematically separated military-aged men from the general population as Kosovars were expelled. These men were detained in facilities ranging from cement factories to prisons. Many of these detainees were forced to dig trenches and were physically abused. At least 2,000 Kosovar Albanians remain in detention in around a dozen Serbian prisons today [December 1999].

- *Summary Executions:* There are accounts of summary executions at about 500 sites across Kosovo.

- *Exhumation of Mass Graves:* Serbian forces burned, destroyed, or exhumed bodies from mass graves in an attempt to destroy evidence. Some were reinterred in individual graves.

- *Rape:* There are numerous accounts indicating that the organized and individual rape of Kosovar Albanian women by Serbian forces was widespread. For example, Serbian forces systematically raped women in Djakovica and Pec, and in some cases rounded up women and took them to hotels where they were raped by troops under encouragement of their commanders. Rape is most likely an underreported atrocity because of the stigma attached to the victims in traditional Kosovar Albanian society.

- *Violations of Medical Neutrality:* Kosovar Albanian physicians, patients and medical facilities were systematically attacked. Many health care facilities were used as protective cover for military activities; NGOs [nongovernmental organizations] report the destruction by Serbian forces of at least 100 clinics, pharmacies, and hospitals.

- *Identity Cleansing:* Kosovar Albanians were systematically stripped of identity and property documents including passports, land titles, automobile license plates, identity cards, and other forms of documentation. As much as 50 percent of the population may be without documentation. By systematically destroying schools, places of worship, and hospitals, Serbian forces sought to destroy social identity and the fabric of Kosovar Albanian society.

- *Aftermath:* Following the withdrawal of Serbian forces in June, Kosovo saw manifestations of a new set of human rights problems. These include acts of retribution against the Serb minority, including the killing of 200–400 Serb residents. In addition, as many as 23,000 conscientious objectors, draft evaders, and deserters in Serbia are threatened with legal action.

## An Account of Atrocities

The following is a general account of atrocities committed by Serbian forces against ethnic Albanians in Kosovo primarily between March 1999 and late June 1999. Most of the information is compiled from victims and witness accounts provided to KFOR, the International Criminal Tribunal for the former Yugoslavia (ICTY), and other international organizations, supplemented by diplomatic and other reporting available as of early November 1999.

Since the signing of the military withdrawal agreement and departure of Serbian forces from Kosovo, earlier reports of Serbian war crimes in Kosovo, including the detention and summary execution of military-aged men and the destruction of civilian housing, have been confirmed by journalists and international organizations. According to press reports, Serbian troops and militias continued to rape women, loot property, burn homes and mosques, and murder Kosovar Albanians while withdrawing from Kosovo. Since the Serbian withdrawal, virtually all Kosovar Albanian survivors have returned to their villages and towns. However, there has also been a mass exodus of Serbian civilians who—despite KFOR efforts to protect them— are fearful of retribution from returning Kosovar Albanians and the influence of former members of the UCK [that is, the Kosovo Liberation Army]. KFOR troops have intervened on numerous occasions to prevent further violence in Kosovo.

War crime investigators and forensic teams from a number of countries and staff of the ICTY have begun investigating the numerous sites of mass graves and mass executions in Kosovo. KFOR has established security at many of the locations of alleged

*Ethnic Albanian refugees are displaced in the mountains of Kosovo. As a result of Serbia's campaign of ethnic cleansing, approximately 90 percent of the Kosovar Albanian population was forcibly expelled from their homes.* © Tyler Hicks/Getty Images News/Getty Images.

atrocities and requested returning family members not to disturb the potential evidence at any of the sites. Many family members choose to rebury their relatives without waiting for forensic investigations, however.

Kosovar Albanians have reported mass executions and mass graves at about 500 sites in the province. As of early November 1999, the ICTY has conducted site investigations at about 200 of these and has confirmed finding bodies at over 160 of the sites. Numerous accounts indicate that Serbian forces took steps to destroy forensic evidence of their crimes. This included execution methods that would allow the Serbs to claim their victims were collateral casualties of military operations, and burning or otherwise disposing of bodies. Over 2,100 bodies have been found by the ICTY among the some 200 atrocity sites that have been field investigated so far. However, the total number of bodies reported to the ICTY at over 500 gravesites is more than 11,000. If the pattern established among these 200 sites holds for all of the remaining sites—claimed by all sources—that have yet to be field investigated, we would expect the total number of bodies to be found at the known gravesites to be over 6,000. To this total must be added three important categories of victims: (1) those buried in mass graves whose locations are unknown, (2) what the ICTY reports is a significant number of sites where the precise number of bodies cannot be counted, and (3) victims whose bodies were burned or destroyed by Serbian forces. Press reporting and eyewitness accounts provide credible details of a program of destruction of evidence by Serbian forces throughout Kosovo and even in Serbia proper. The number of victims whose bodies have been burned or destroyed may never be known, but enough evidence has emerged to conclude that probably around 10,000 Kosovar Albanians were killed by Serbian forces.

## Expulsion and Rape

As a result of Serbian efforts to expel the ethnic Albanian majority from Kosovo, almost one million Kosovar Albanians left the province after Serbian forces launched their first security crackdown in March 1998, with most having fled after March 1999. Based on the scope and intensity of Serbian activities throughout the province, as many as 500,000 additional Kosovars appear to have been internally displaced. In sum, about 1.5 million Kosovar Albanians (at least 90 percent of the estimated 1998 Kosovar Albanian population of the province) were forcibly expelled from their homes. Virtually all Kosovar Albanians who desired to return to Kosovo have done so at this time.

Thousands of homes in at least 1,200 cities, towns, and villages were damaged or destroyed. Victims report that Serbian forces harassed them with forced extortion and beatings, and that some were strafed by Serbian aircraft. Reports of organized rape of ethnic Albanian women by Serbian security forces during the conflict continue to be received. According to the victims, Serbian forces conducted systematic rapes in Djakovica, and at the Karagac and Metohia hotels in Pec.

With the return of international organizations to Kosovo in late June 1999, an unambiguous picture has unfolded, showing the scope and intensity of the ethnic cleansing campaign waged in the province.

Refugees have reported that Serbian forces systematically separated military-aged ethnic Albanian men—ranging from as young as age 14 years to 59 years old—from the population as they expelled the Kosovar Albanians from their homes. An exact accounting of the number of men killed is impossible because of Serbian efforts to destroy bodies of their victims, but clearly it includes civilians, combatants who were killed while prisoners of war as defined under the laws of armed conflict, and combatants killed while participating in hostilities. Forensic investigations will provide some, but not all, of the answers as to the relative proportions of each category.

# The NATO Air Campaign in Serbia Begins

*The Economist*

*The* Economist *is a British news and business publication. In the following viewpoint, the authors report on the decision by NATO, the North Atlantic Treaty Organization, to begin bombing Serbia in March 1999. The* Economist *says that the decision to attack was based on Serbian atrocities in Kosovo, including mass killings and forced expulsion of Kosovar Albanians. According to the* Economist, *it is unclear whether NATO intends the bombings as a warning or as the beginning of war. The* Economist *notes, however, that the situation could quickly escalate, either by provoking Serb retaliation or by encouraging attacks by Albanians on Serbs.*

Just ten days short of its 50th anniversary, the Atlantic alliance has gone into battle with a medium-sized European country, while vowing to protect all other states in the neighbourhood from the fall-out. Instead of starting with pin-pricks, dozens of NATO [North Atlantic Treaty Organization] aircraft began a spectacular bombing campaign on the night of March 24th [1999] with raids on airfields and arms factories near Belgrade, Serbia's capital, and targets near Pristina, capital of Serbia's already battered southern province of Kosovo. Cruise missiles were launched from air and sea. Bombs also fell on Montenegro—Serbia's reluctant junior partner in the rump state of Yugoslavia—dashing its hopes of being spared. NATO raids continued on March 25th.

## Warnings and War

Earlier in the week, Javier Solana, the NATO secretary-general, had promised on the allies' behalf to "disrupt" Yugoslavia's war against Kosovo's ethnic Albanians and their villages. The scale of the latest repression ordered by Yugoslavia's president, Slobodan Milosevic, convinced even NATO's doubters—France, for one—that something had to be done. His forces have uprooted at least 65,000 people in the past month, bringing to 250,000 the number now homeless in Kosovo.

But right from the start there was confusion about NATO's precise purpose and legal justification. As the bombs started falling, [US] President Bill Clinton said the raids were intended to demonstrate NATO's "opposition to aggression"; to deter further attacks on civilians; and "if necessary" to damage Serbia's capacity to make war. In other words, the first wave of bombs was intended as a warning—and only if it were ignored would NATO start seriously destroying the Yugoslav arsenal.

Mr Solana, for his part, suggested that Serbia was being punished for its refusal to accept a settlement in Kosovo and let NATO police it. He also stressed, however, that the alliance "was not waging war against Yugoslavia" and had no quarrel with its (mainly Serb) people. In practice, the distinction between warnings and war could vanish from sight if the conflict develops into a broader test of wills between the western alliance and Serbia's power-broker. NATO's trump cards include vast firepower and fairly solid unity of purpose in its own ranks. Mr Milosevic, for his part, will be banking on his own people's greater willingness to accept and inflict casualties—and on the fact that all nations, even exhausted and divided ones, tend to rally round the flag when under attack.

The Yugoslav government (which formally speaks for Serbia and an increasingly restive Montenegro) has given grim warnings to Romania, Albania, Bulgaria, Hungary and Macedonia not to take part "directly or indirectly" in any NATO actions. Of these countries, only Hungary (one of three ex-communist ones to join the alliance last month) is covered by NATO's mutual defence guarantee. But NATO has told the other four—plus Slovenia—that it would view a Yugoslav attack on them very gravely. The reassurance is timely: Macedonia is host to 12,000 NATO troops, in range of Serbian artillery fire.

## Increasing Repression

As NATO's aircraft revved up their engines, the Yugoslav leader's first moves were to complete a purge of the security forces, and silence the voices of domestic opposition. The army's intelligence chief was replaced by someone even more loyal; this, combined with the replacement in recent months of the heads of both the armed forces and the secret service, will dampen western hopes of a palace coup.

As Belgrade's few remaining lights of independence went out, a dissident radio station, B-92, was shut down. Mr Milosevic can certainly count, at least initially, on support among his fellow Serbs. Most have no idea of the scale of the refugee crisis, or the atrocities committed by their police; many regard Kosovo as a symbol of their history and faith. On the other hand, Serbia's propaganda has kept many citizens so cocooned from reality that nobody can predict how they will react when they realise NATO is not bluffing this time.

Serbia's forces are the rusting but still serviceable remnants of an army that was built up during the cold war as a defender of Yugoslavia's non-aligned status.[1] As well as buying Soviet-made aircraft and air-defences, the communist state made aircraft, tanks and ships of its own.

A well-integrated network of surface-to-air missile launchers, including the mobile SA-6, which brought down an American

"1 mile to Kosovo," cartoon by Angonoa, www.CartoonStock.com. Copyright © Angonoa. Reproduction rights obtainable from www.CartoonStock.com.

aircraft over Bosnia in 1995, means that western bombers will have a harder time weaving through the Serbian skies than they do when swooping over Iraq.[2] "In Bosnia, the Serbs proved to be skilled at electronic warfare," says a British missile-watcher. "They could tell when NATO aircraft were targeting their air-defence sites with anti-radar missiles, and switched off their radar in time to avoid destruction."

NATO's war plan therefore calls for the firing of at least 100 cruise missiles, based at sea or off B-52 aircraft, to mess up the Serbs' air defenses. Because these projectiles have satellite-based guidance, they should be even "smarter" than they were during the Gulf war [against Iraq, 1990–1991]. More accurate still—so long as the weather is good—are the laser-guided bombs that America's stealthy F-117 bombers may unleash. And another stealthy giant, the B-2, is having its war-debut. If NATO singles out the heavy armour that is wrecking Kosovo's villages, it can call on the A-10 "tank-buster" aircraft.

Some veteran Balkan observers believe the Belgrade regime could crumble as popular anger over the corruption and cynicism of Mr Milosevic's circle replaces patriotic fervour. In Kosovo, though, events could spin out of all control. The rebels of the loosely knit Kosovo Liberation Army may use any opportunity provided by NATO firepower to take revenge on Serb civilians. Another worry is that any restraint Serbia might exercise on its special forces and paramilitary units could be lost if communication systems are destroyed by bombing. And [the capital of Kosovo] Pristina's warren of hillside settlements and communist-era apartment buildings could become another Beirut.[3]

## Notes

1. Serbia was part of Communist Yugoslavia until the disintegration of Yugoslavia in the early 1990s.
2. Western forces patrolled the air in Iraq in the 1990s after the first Gulf War.
3. Lebanon was war-torn through the 1970s and 1980s.

# Albanians Commit Ethnic Cleansing Against Kosovo Serbs

*Robert Fisk*

*Robert Fisk is a British journalist and writer and the Middle East correspondent for the* Independent. *In the following viewpoint, he reports that NATO has ended the Serb attack on Kosovo, and Albanians have returned to the province. However, he says, Albanians are murdering and harassing ethnic minorities in Kosovo. He says that Serbs, Jews, Croats, and other minorities have been targeted for killing, and large numbers of them have been forced to flee Kosovo. Fisk argues that NATO, which intervened on behalf of the Albanians in Kosovo, has done little to protect the minorities in the region.*

The postwar "ethnic cleansing" of Kosovo's Serbs appears to be nearing completion as armed Albanians continue to murder and kidnap the tiny minority of Serbs who remain in the province more than five months after NATO [North Atlantic Treaty Organization] troops arrived—in the words of their UN mandate—"to ensure public safety and order." Of [Kosovo capital] Pristina's 40,000 Serb population, only 400 are left. Statistics

## Attacks on Serbs and Others

Ethnic violence in Kosovo did not halt with the end of the international conflict, the withdrawal of Serb forces, the deployment of NATO troops and the UN Mission, or the return of Kosovar refugees. This continued violence has affected both sides, but proportionally the Serbs and other minorities have suffered most heavily. Serbs have been subjected to kidnapping, murder, arson, grenade attacks, shootings, and a variety of other intimidation tactics, including bombing places of worship. NGOs [nongovernmental organizations] have also recently documented abuses against Serb patients in hospitals in Kosovo and intimidation of Serb physicians.

Since June 10 [1999], between 200 and 400 Serb residents of Kosovo have been killed, thousands of Serb homes and apartments have been torched, destroyed, or looted, and according to Serbian Orthodox Church officials, more than 40 Serbian Orthodox churches and monasteries have been damaged or destroyed. In one of the worst incidents, on July 23, 1999, 14 Serb farmers were killed while working their fields near the village of Gracko. On August 11, an international forensic team completed a site inves-

from the Serb church and a human rights group in Pristina suggest as many as 316 Serbs have been murdered and 455 more kidnapped, many of them killed, since NATO's arrival.

## Serbs Are Unprotected

If these figures bear any relation to reality—and most are accompanied by names and dates—then the number of Serbs killed in the five months since the war comes close to that of Albanians murdered by Serbs in the five months before NATO began its bombardment in March [1999].[1]

Most Serb victims died in the first two months after NATO's entry, but house-burning and murder continues. One of the most recent deaths was that of a Serb restaurant worker employed—by tigation at Llapushnica and confirmed finding a mass grave containing seven bodies. While none of the bodies had been positively identified at that time, preliminary indications suggest that the victims were Serbs.

The Roma population has also been the focus of retribution, being accused of collaborating in the expulsion of Kosovar Albanians. Historical animosity against the Roma community has also played a role. A July 20 statement condemning attacks on Serbs and Roma was released by the former UCK [Kosovo Liberation Army] leadership, and former UCK leader Hashim Thaqi publicly denounced the July 23 Gracko attack. There is no evidence that the former UCK leadership is orchestrating the violence. On the other hand, Kosovar Albanians have neither identified the perpetrators of these crimes, nor has the condemnation of these abuses by leaders of the Kosovar Albanian population been as broad, sustained, or effective as the circumstances warrant.

Prior to 1999, there were an estimated 200,000 Serbs in Kosovo. Today, some 97,000 remain, according to KFOR [NATO forces in Kosovo].

*US Department of State,* Ethnic Cleansing in Kosovo: An Accounting, *December 1999.*
*www.state.gov.*

a supreme irony—at the Pristina office of the International War Crimes Tribunal. The murder of Radovan Kukalj in his home town of Obilic on 29 October went almost unreported outside Kosovo.

Statistics compiled by the NATO-led K-For [Kosovo force] in Kosovo appear to be woefully inaccurate. They give the number of Serbs murdered since mid-June as only 125, despite detailed lists from the Serb Orthodox Diocese of Raska and Prizren that include at least 184 named Serbs as murder victims, and a further 104 kidnapped between 13 June and 22 August alone.

Files at the Serbian-administered "Centre for Peace and Tolerance" in Pristina—which includes Albanian victims in its statistics—say that at least 48 Albanians as well as 455 Serbs have been kidnapped since mid-June.

*A widow is comforted at a funeral following the 1999 Gracko massacre, one of the worst attacks against Serbs after Albanians returned to Kosovo.* © AP Images/David Brauchli.

But even if the true figure was closer to K-For's statistic, not one of the brutal Serb killings is being investigated by members of the International War Crimes Tribunal working in Kosovo, not even the death of their own restaurant worker, Mr Kukalj. For while tribunal investigators still hope to bring charges against the murderers of Albanians killed before the war, they are prevented by the tribunal's mandate from any detective work on the postwar murder of Serbs.

## Minorities Flee

The mandate states that it can investigate crimes committed "during the armed conflict in Kosovo". But since neither NATO nor K-For will admit that a conflict continues under their control in Kosovo, albeit a largely one-sided one in which the Serbs are the principal victims, war crimes tribunal officials cannot investigate the killing of Serbs. This means their murderers have only the largely impotent UN police force to reckon with. No wonder, then, that minority groups continue to flee Kosovo.

The 300-strong Croat community at Lecnice were preparing to celebrate their 700th anniversary in the province but left en masse last month for Dubrovnik [in Croatia]. And this week, the president of the tiny Jewish community in Pristina, Cedra Prlincevic, left for Belgrade [Serbia] after denouncing "a pogrom against the non-Albanian population". He had left Kosovo, he said, "with only the Talmud" [a Jewish religious text].

Foreign aid workers in Kosovo insist K-For is now making a huge effort to protect minorities after NATO General Sir Michael Jackson's defeatist response to the killings—"we can only do so much," he said several times—appeared to encourage the killers.

"There are large numbers of Royal Irish Rangers in the Gjilane and Stimle areas trying to defend the small number of Serbs there," a European human rights worker said. "Just east of Pec, Serbs are returning from Montenegro [a country bordering Serbia and Kosovo] at the rate of 40 a week and K-For is putting enormous resources in to re-establish them."

Swedish troops have virtually surrounded the Serb monastery town of Gracanica, even ordering Albanians to strip Kosovo independence posters from their cars if they are driving in the Serb streets.

But the same aid official, who spends much of his time on emergency work in Pristina, admitted: "Every single Serbian here has been intimidated—verbally in the street, on the telephone, physically . . ."

A few hours later, I was confronted by a 64-year-old Serb woman, Milunka Josic, who had just spent the night trying to keep Albanian youths from breaking down her front door. Her right hand was covered in bruises. "I know the young men who were shouting at me," she said. "They were beating on the door and screaming, '**** your mother' and, 'Go back to Serbia.'"

## Harassment Continues

In efforts to minimise the "ethnic cleansing" of the Serbs of Kosovo, K-For has even produced graphs which compare the province favourably to cities which include Pretoria and Moscow, a meaningless performance since these are among the crime capitals of the world. But human rights teams of the OSCE [Organization for Security and Co-operation in Europe], who work with the UN police force, say they are investigating "an increasing number of murders, attacks and harassment of elderly Serbs".

An OSCE official reports that in Zupa, a 96-year-old Serb man was found bound and gagged with a gunshot wound to the head. He had been gathering food for a small community of Serbs who were too frightened to visit the local Albanian-run grocery store. In Kamenica, an 82-year-old Serb woman—who had been threatened and ordered to move from her house, was found burnt to death in her home.

Earlier, Serbs reported that a 90-year-old woman, Ljubica Vujovic, had been held down in her bathtub and drowned. Elderly Kosovo Albanians also complain that Albanian families burnt out of their original homes by Serbs are trying to evict them. Witnesses, say the OSCE, are too fearful to help the UN and K-For investigate these crimes.

Amid this anarchy, the question has to be asked: can the shameful campaign of "ethnic cleansing" and murder of Serbs that continues under K-For's eyes still be explained away as revenge attacks, as retaliation for the mass atrocities committed against Albanians by Serb forces before and during the Kosovo war?

## Serbs Out

A growing number of Albanian intellectuals, including several courageous journalists on the daily *Koha Ditore* newspaper, fear that the murders and dispossession of Serbs are now being organised. By who? By KLA [Kosovo Liberation Army] cells that never disbanded under K-For orders? By groups coming across the border from Albania?

Serbs, of course, still remember a British minister saying during the Kosovo war that he wanted "Serbs out, NATO in, refugees back". George Robertson, as Secretary of State for Defence, later claimed this was merely a "distillation" of the G8 [a forum for eight major economic powers] demands.

But "Serbs Out" has almost been accomplished. Mr Robertson is now head of NATO.

## Note

1. Killings of Albanians intensified in the period after the NATO bombing began.

# Serbian Leader Dies in Custody at the International Criminal Tribunal

*Kevin Parker*

*Kevin Parker was a judge at the International Criminal Tribunal for the Former Yugoslavia in 2006. In the following viewpoint, he reports on the result of his investigation into the death of former Serbian President Slobodan Milosevic while in custody at the International Criminal Court. Parker discusses the war crimes charges against Milosevic for his role in wars in Croatia, Bosnia, and Kosovo. Parker says that Milosevic's health had long been weak and seriously affected the conduct of his trials. Milosevic insisted on defending himself and required frequent delays and adjournments. Parker reports that Milosevic died in his cell as the result of natural causes before the completion of his trial.*

Slobodan Milošević [former president of Serbia] died in his cell at the United Nations Detention Unit ("UNDU") in the Scheveningen Penitentiary Facility on Saturday morning, 11 March 2006. The time of death has not been conclusively determined. Standard assessment suggests around 0745 hours. The

Kevin Parker, "Report to the President: Death of Slobodan Milosevic," International Criminal Tribunal for the Former Yugoslavia, May 2006. www.icty.org. Copyright © 2006 by United Nations. Reprinted with the permission of the United Nations.

post mortem report indicates between 0700 and 0900 hours. He was alone in the locked cell.

## Death by Natural Causes

Coronial and police investigations, under the aegis of the District Office of the Public Prosecutor in The Hague [in the Netherlands, where war crime trials are conducted], have been undertaken. These include a very detailed autopsy, including full pathological and toxicological investigations, conducted by the Netherlands Forensic Institute.

Despite allegations, which received much attention in some segments of the media, that he was the victim of murder, especially by poisoning, these investigations have confirmed that Mr. Milošević died of natural causes from a heart attack and that there was no poison or other chemical substance found in his body that contributed to the death.

This Inquiry relies on the reports and findings of those investigations, which were conducted entirely independently of this Tribunal. There has also been an independent audit of UNDU by a specialist Swedish Team.

## Events of March 11, 2006

Slobodan Milošević was detained in the E1 wing of UNDU. At 0900 hours on Saturday, 11 March 2006, two guards unlocked the cells of E1 wing. On weekends cells are usually unlocked at the later time of 0900 hours and those detainees who wish to go out to the exercise yard for sport are taken out for an hour. A guard opened Mr. Milošević's cell and called "Good Morning!" but heard no response. He saw that Mr. Milošević was lying on his bed and assumed that he was still asleep. Mr. Milošević did not usually participate in the outdoor sport sessions, but on weekends he would normally be awake at 0900 hours and would be given his medications. The guard left Mr. Milošević's cell open while he gave medications to some other detainees in the wing. As Mr. Milošević had not stirred the guard decided to give Mr. Milošević his medications later when he woke. At about 0905 hours the two guards locked the cells of all detainees on El wing who did not go to sport, including that of Mr. Milošević, and left the floor with the detainees going to sport. The actions of the guard in not taking a closer look at Mr. Milosevic cannot be fairly criticised in the circumstances as they presented themselves to the guard at the time. In particular, as will be apparent later in this Report, the need for Mr. Milošević to rest at weekends was by then a significant feature of the management of his health.

At 1005 hours sport was finished and the two guards returned with their detainees to El wing. The two guards then once again opened all cells. One of the guards looked through the observation window into the cell of Mr. Milošević and saw that he was still lying on his bed. The guard unlocked the door and entered the cell. As he approached the bed he saw that Mr. Milošević's face was greyish in colour and that his arm was hanging over the side of the bed. His face muscles were sunken and his ears were blue. The guard summoned a colleague from the guardroom. Together they sought to confirm whether Mr. Milošević was dead. The second guard called Mr. Milošević by name, shook his foot and tried in vain to detect any pulse beat. There was no response. It was apparent to both guards that Mr. Milošević had died.

The guards then left the cell, locking the door, telephoned the shift supervisor, who was in the control booth, informed him of the situation and asked him to make all necessary telephone calls. Two other guards immediately ran from the control booth to confirm that Mr. Milošević was dead. The shift supervisor called the Commanding Officer of UNDU, his deputy and the medical officer, Dr Falke. No signs of life could be found. The guards then left the cell and again locked the door while waiting for the doctor. Meanwhile, other guards returned all detainees

*Photo on following page: Anti–Slobodan Milosevic activists celebrate the funeral of the former Serbian president on the streets of Belgrade in 2006.* © AP Images/Petar Petrov.

on the wing and the adjacent wing back to their cells and locked the doors.

By about 1030 hours Dr Falke arrived at UNDU. He went immediately to Mr. Milošević's cell accompanied by a guard and confirmed the death of Mr. Milošević. The cell door was then locked and sealed. The Dutch police had also been informed and arrived at UNDU shortly after Dr Falke. They immediately pursued their various inquiries, including interviewing Dr Falke and all guards who were on duty. Two detectives, three forensic experts, and Haaglanden uniformed police officers attended at UNDU. The sealed door to Mr. Milošević's cell was unsealed to allow access by the Dutch police.

Further Dutch police officers arrived and two coroners. At 1615 hours two Dutch municipal coroners conducted an external examination of the body of Mr. Milošević. At about 1800 hours, after consultations with the Tribunal's Registrar, the Dutch Public Prosecutor ordered that Mr. Milošević's body is taken into custody and that a full forensic autopsy be conducted.

At about 1910 hours Mr. Milošević's body was removed from E1 wing and later was transported to the Netherlands Forensic Institute. The cell of Mr. Milošević was sealed by the Dutch police after the removal of his body.

## Background and Trial

Slobodan Milošević was born on 20 August 1941 in Pozarevac, in the present-day Republic of Serbia. He began his political career in 1983 and from 1984 to 1988 he held various leadership positions within the League of Communists of Serbia. On 16 July 1990, after the creation of the Socialist Party of Serbia, Mr. Milošević became its President and held this post until 2001. In May 1989 Mr. Milošević became the President of Serbia and in July 1997 he was elected the President of the Federal Republic of Yugoslavia. Following defeat in the September 2000 Presidential elections, on 6 October 2000 Mr. Milošević was forced to step down.

Slobodan Milošević was initially indicted before this Tribunal on 24 May 1999 for crimes against humanity and war crimes committed in the territory of Kosovo after January 1999. On 8 October 2001 he was also indicted for crimes against humanity and war crimes committed in Croatia between August 1991 and June 1992. On 22 November 2001 he was further charged with genocide, crimes against humanity, and war crimes committed in the territory of Bosnia and Herzegovina from 1 March 1992 until 31 December 1995. On 27 November 2001 the Office of the Prosecutor ("Prosecution") moved for joinder of the three Indictments against Slobodan Milošević. On 13 December 2001 the Trial Chamber joined the Croatia and Bosnia Indictments but ordered that the Kosovo Indictment be tried separately. On 1 February 2002 the Appeals Chamber reversed the decision of the Trial Chamber and ordered that the three Indictments be tried in one trial.

Slobodan Milošević was transferred to UNDU on 29 June 2001. He adamantly insisted on representing himself in all pre-trial proceedings and in the trial which commenced on 12 February 2002. He was entitled to do so under Article 21(4)(d) of the Statute of the Tribunal. He did so despite often repeated medical advice that it was dangerous for him to bear the burden and stress of representing himself. In the course of the presentation of its case, which continued until 25 February 2004, the Prosecution called 352 witnesses. The evidence of some 200 of them was presented, fully or partly, in the form of written statements.

## Interruptions Due to Health

The trial was interrupted frequently during the Prosecution case because of Mr. Milošević's health. In August 2002 the trial schedule was reduced, on the recommendation of the cardiologist treating Mr. Milošević, Dr van Dijkman, to allow four consecutive days of rest every two weeks of trial. This was further reduced in September 2003 on the advice of Dr van Dijkman to a trial schedule of only three sitting days a week. This schedule remained basically in place until the termination of the proceedings, although on numerous occasions additional adjournments were granted, either or both because of the health of Mr. Milošević or to allow him additional preparation time. Altogether 66 trial days were lost during the Prosecution case because of the health of Mr. Milošević.

The Defence case was initially scheduled to begin three months after the close of the Prosecution case. Nevertheless, the start of the Defence case had to be postponed on five occasions on the account of Mr. Milošević's ill-health. The conduct of the trial was further affected by the resignation because of ill-health of the Presiding Judge and the appointment of a new Judge to the bench.

The case for Mr. Milošević commenced on 31 August 2004. On 2 September 2004, in view of detailed medical reports it had received regarding Mr. Milošević's health, the Trial Chamber made an order assigning counsel to Mr. Milošević. The effect of the modalities provided by that order would have been that the assigned defence counsel would have primary responsibility for conducting and presenting the defence case. The modalities of this order were reversed by the Appeals Chamber in November 2004, returning the effective conduct and presentation of the defence case to Mr. Milošević. Despite the availability to him of assigned counsel he continued to present his case in court and was heavily involved in the ongoing preparation of his witnesses and his case.

Over a year later, on 12 December 2005, in court session, Slobodan Milošević requested to be provisionally released to Russia for health reasons. On 23 February 2006 the Trial Chamber denied Mr. Milošević's request. An appeal against this decision was filed by Mr. Milošević on 2 March 2006 but this had not been heard when he died nine days later.

On 8, 9, and 10 March 2006 the trial again stood adjourned, this time to enable Mr. Milošević to proof Mr. Momir Bulatović, the President of the Republic of Montenegro at times relevant to the Indictment, who was about to testify for Mr. Milošević in the trial. The death of Mr. Milošević on Saturday 11 March 2006 brought the trial to a premature end. At the time of his death the trial was drawing to a close. The trial schedule was for the defence evidence to conclude in May 2006.

# Kosovo Declares Independence

*Assembly of Kosovo*

*The Kosovo Declaration of Independence is the official establishment of an independent Kosovo nation by the Kosovo government and people. In this viewpoint, Kosovo declares itself a member of the international community and promises to fulfill its diplomatic and treaty obligations. It commits to being a multiethnic state without violence against minorities and expresses a wish to join the European Union. It also states that it will be a good neighbor to adjoining states and expresses a desire for good relations with Serbia, the country from which it is declaring independence.*

Convened in an extraordinary meeting on February 17, 2008, in Pristina, the capital of Kosovo,

*Answering* the call of the people to build a society that honors human dignity and affirms the pride and purpose of its citizens,

*Committed* to confront the painful legacy of the recent past in a spirit of reconciliation and forgiveness,

*Dedicated* to protecting, promoting and honoring the diversity of our people,

"Kosovo Declaration of Independence," Assembly of Kosovo, February 17, 2008. www .assembly-kosova.org.

*Reaffirming* our wish to become fully integrated into the Euro-Atlantic family of democracies,

*Observing* that Kosovo is a special case arising from Yugoslavia's non-consensual breakup and is not a precedent for any other situation,

*Recalling* the years of strife and violence in Kosovo, that disturbed the conscience of all civilised people,

*Grateful* that in 1999 the world intervened, thereby removing Belgrade's [the Serbian capital's] governance over Kosovo and placing Kosovo under United Nations interim administration,

*Proud* that Kosovo has since developed functional, multiethnic institutions of democracy that express freely the will of our citizens,

*Recalling* the years of internationally-sponsored negotiations between Belgrade and Pristina [the capital of Kosovo] over the question of our future political status,

*Regretting* that no mutually-acceptable status outcome was possible, in spite of the good-faith engagement of our leaders,

*Confirming* that the recommendations of UN Special Envoy Martti Ahtisaari provide Kosovo with a comprehensive framework for its future development and are in line with the highest European standards of human rights and good governance,

*Determined* to see our status resolved in order to give our people clarity about their future, move beyond the conflicts of the past and realise the full democratic potential of our society,

*Honoring* all the men and women who made great sacrifices to build a better future for Kosovo,

Approves

## Kosova Declaration of Independence

1. We, the democratically-elected leaders of our people, hereby declare Kosovo to be an independent and sovereign state. This declaration reflects the will of our people and it is in full accordance with the

*In February 2008, Kosovars celebrate the independence of Kosovo from Serbia by displaying the new nation's flag.* © Daniel Mihailescu/AFP/Getty Images.

recommendations of UN Special Envoy Martti Ahtisaari and his Comprehensive Proposal for the Kosovo Status Settlement.

2. We declare Kosovo to be a democratic, secular and multi-ethnic republic, guided by the principles of non-discrimination and equal protection under the law. We shall protect and promote the rights of all communities in Kosovo and create the conditions necessary for their effective participation in political and decision-making processes.

3. We accept fully the obligations for Kosovo contained in the Ahtisaari Plan, and welcome the framework it proposes to guide Kosovo in the years ahead. We shall implement in full those obligations including through priority adoption of the legislation included in its Annex XII, particularly those that protect and promote the rights of communities and their members.

4. We shall adopt as soon as possible a Constitution that enshrines our commitment to respect the human rights and fundamental freedoms of all our citizens, particularly as defined by the European Convention on Human Rights. The Constitution shall incorporate all relevant principles of the Ahtisaari Plan and be adopted through a democratic and deliberative process.

5. We welcome the international community's continued support of our democratic development through international presences established in Kosovo on the basis of UN Security Council resolution 1244 (1999).[1] We invite and welcome an international civilian presence to supervise our implementation of the Ahtisaari Plan, and a European Union–led rule of law mission. We also invite and welcome the North Atlantic Treaty Organization to retain the leadership role of the international military presence in Kosovo and to implement responsibilities assigned to it under UN Security Council resolution 1244 (1999) and the Ahtisaari Plan, until such time as Kosovo institutions are capable of assuming these responsibilities. We shall cooperate fully with these presences to ensure Kosovo's future peace, prosperity and stability.

6. For reasons of culture, geography and history, we believe our future lies with the European family. We therefore declare our intention to take all steps necessary to facilitate full membership in the European Union [an economic and political union of European states] as soon as feasible

and implement the reforms required for European and Euro-Atlantic integration.

7. We express our deep gratitude to the United Nations for the work it has done to help us recover and rebuild from war and build institutions of democracy. We are committed to working constructively with the United Nations as it continues its work in the period ahead.

8. With independence comes the duty of responsible membership in the international community. We accept fully this duty and shall abide by the principles of the United Nations Charter, the Helsinki Final Act [which provides for state sovereignty and cooperation in Europe], other acts of the Organization on Security and Cooperation in Europe, and the international legal obligations and principles of international comity that mark the relations among states. Kosovo shall have its international borders as set forth in Annex VIII of the Ahtisaari Plan, and shall fully respect the sovereignty and territorial integrity of all our neighbors. Kosovo shall also refrain from the threat or use of force in any manner inconsistent with the purposes of the United Nations.

9. We hereby undertake the international obligations of Kosovo, including those concluded on our behalf by the United Nations Interim Administration Mission in Kosovo (UNMIK) and treaty and other obligations of the former Socialist Federal Republic of Yugoslavia to which we are bound as a former constituent part, including the Vienna Conventions on diplomatic and consular relations.[2] We shall cooperate fully with the International Criminal Tribunal for the Former Yugoslavia [which investigated war crimes in Kosovo]. We intend to seek membership in international organisations, in which Kosovo shall seek to contribute to the pursuit of international peace and stability.

10. Kosovo declares its commitment to peace and stability in our region of southeast Europe. Our independence brings to an end the process of Yugoslavia's violent dissolution. While this process has been a painful one, we shall work tirelessly to contribute to a reconciliation that would allow southeast Europe to move beyond the conflicts of our past and forge new links of regional cooperation. We shall therefore work together with our neighbours to advance a common European future.

11. We express, in particular, our desire to establish good relations with all our neighbours, including the Republic of Serbia with whom we have deep historical, commercial and social ties that we seek to develop further in the near future. We shall continue our efforts to contribute to relations of friendship and cooperation with the Republic of Serbia, while promoting reconciliation among our people.

12. We hereby affirm, clearly, specifically, and irrevocably, that Kosovo shall be legally bound to comply with the provisions contained in this Declaration, including, especially, the obligations for it under the Ahtisaari Plan. In all of these matters, we shall act consistent with principles of international law and resolutions of the Security Council of the United Nations, including resolution 1244 (1999). We declare publicly that all states are entitled to rely upon this declaration, and appeal to them to extend to us their support and friendship.

## Notes

1. UN Security Council resolution 1244 called for the end of Serbian aggression in Kosovo in 1999.
2. The Vienna Conventions on diplomatic and consular relations established the framework that allows diplomats to perform their functions without harassment.

# CHAPTER 2

# Controversies Surrounding Kosovo

# Chapter Exercises

"Serbia Versus Kosovo," cartoon by Peter Welleman, www.CartoonStock.com. Copyright © Peter Welleman. Reproduction rights obtainable from www.CartoonStock.com.

## 1. Analyze the Cartoon

**Question 1:** Is this cartoon pro-Serbia or anti-Serbia? What evidence is there in the cartoon to support your conclusion?

**Question 2:** Was this cartoon created before or after NATO intervened in the Serbian conflict? What evidence supports your conclusion?

**Question 3:** What do the relative sizes of NATO, Serbia, and Kosovo tell you about the relative strength or size of each?

## 2. Writing Prompt

Imagine that you are writing an essay for an online magazine on the anniversary of the end of the Kosovo conflict. Write an editorial in which you argue that the events in Kosovo either *were* genocide or *were not* genocide. Be sure to define what you mean by genocide and to explain why you believe the events in Kosovo did or did not fit that definition.

## 3. Group Activity

Form groups and support or refute the following statement: The Milosevic trial showed that international war crime trials can be successful in advancing justice and healing.

# Serbia Has Created a Humanitarian Disaster in Kosovo

*Bill Clinton*

*Bill Clinton was the president of the United States from 1992 to 2000. In the following viewpoint, he argues that Serbia is using military force against civilians in Kosovo. He says that the Kosovar Albanians have agreed to a peace deal, but Slobodan Milosevic, the Serb leader, has rejected it. He also argues that Serbian aggression threatens to create a refugee crisis throughout southeastern Europe that may engulf important US allies like Greece. Clinton adds that if the United States and NATO do not act with airstrikes against Serb forces, the credibility of NATO's authority will be called into question. Clinton concludes that to protect civilian lives and safeguard the security of Europe, the United States must push back against Serbian aggression.*

My fellow Americans, today [March 24, 1999] our Armed Forces joined our NATO allies in airstrikes against Serbian forces responsible for the brutality in Kosovo. We have acted with resolve for several reasons.

Bill Clinton, "Statement on Kosovo," Miller Center of Public Affairs, University of Virginia, March 24, 1999. www.MillerCenter.org.

We act to protect thousands of innocent people in Kosovo from a mounting military offensive. We act to prevent a wider war, to diffuse a powder keg at the heart of Europe that has exploded twice before in this century with catastrophic results. And we act to stand united with our allies for peace. By acting now, we are upholding our values, protecting our interests, and advancing the cause of peace.

## Advancing the Cause of Peace

Tonight I want to speak to you about the tragedy in Kosovo and why it matters to America that we work with our allies to end it. First, let me explain what it is we are responding to. Kosovo is a province of Serbia, in the middle of southeastern Europe, about 160 miles east of Italy. That's less than the distance between Washington and New York and only about 70 miles north of Greece. Its people are mostly ethnic Albanian and mostly Muslim.

In 1989 Serbia's leader, Slobodan Milosevic, the same leader who started the wars in Bosnia and Croatia and moved against Slovenia in the last decade [the 1990s], stripped Kosovo of the constitutional autonomy its people enjoyed, thus denying them their right to speak their language, run their schools, shape their daily lives. For years, Kosovars struggled peacefully to get their rights back. When President Milosevic sent his troops and police to crush them, the struggle grew violent.

Last fall our diplomacy, backed by the threat of force from our NATO [North Atlantic Treaty Organization] alliance, stopped the fighting for a while and rescued tens of thousands of people from freezing and starvation in the hills where they had fled to save their lives. And last month, with our allies and Russia, we proposed a peace agreement to end the fighting for good. The Kosovar leaders signed that agreement last week. Even though it does not give them all they want, even though their people were still being savaged, they saw that a just peace is better than a long and unwinnable war.

## Serbians Refuse the Treaty

The Serbian leaders, on the other hand, refused even to discuss key elements of the peace agreement. As the Kosovars were saying yes to peace, Serbia stationed 40,000 troops in and around Kosovo in preparation for a major offensive—and in clear violation of the commitments they had made.

Now they've started moving from village to village, shelling civilians and torching their houses. We've seen innocent people taken from their homes, forced to kneel in the dirt, and sprayed with bullets; Kosovar men dragged from their families, fathers and sons together, lined up and shot in cold blood. This is not war in the traditional sense. It is an attack by tanks and artillery on a largely defenseless people whose leaders already have agreed to peace.

Ending this tragedy is a moral imperative. It is also important to America's national interest. . . . Kosovo is a small place, but it sits on a major fault line between Europe, Asia, and the Middle East, at the meeting place of Islam and both the Western and Orthodox branches of Christianity. To the south are our allies, Greece and Turkey; to the north, our new democratic allies in central Europe. And all around Kosovo there are other small countries struggling with their own economic and political challenges, countries that could be overwhelmed by a large, new wave of refugees from Kosovo. All the ingredients for a major war are there: ancient grievances, struggling democracies, and in the center of it all a dictator in Serbia who has done nothing since the cold war[1] ended but start new wars and pour gasoline on the flames of ethnic and religious division.

Sarajevo, the capital of neighboring Bosnia, is where World War I began. World War II and the Holocaust engulfed this region. In both wars, Europe was slow to recognize the dangers, and

***Photo on following page:*** *Addressing NATO troops in April 1999, US president Bill Clinton commends their campaign which forced Serbian troops to withdraw from Kosovo.* © Cynthia Johnson/Getty Images News/Getty Images.

the United States waited even longer to enter the conflicts. Just imagine if leaders back then had acted wisely and early enough, how many lives could have been saved, how many Americans would not have had to die.

## An Atrocity in Europe

We learned some of the same lessons in Bosnia just a few years ago. The world did not act early enough to stop that war, either. And let's not forget what happened: innocent people herded into concentration camps, children gunned down by snipers on their way to school, soccer fields and parks turned into cemeteries, a quarter of a million people killed, not because of anything they have done but because of who they were. Two million Bosnians became refugees. This was genocide in the heart of Europe, not in 1945 but in 1995; not in some grainy newsreel from our parents' and grandparents' time but in our own time, testing our humanity and our resolve.

At the time, many people believed nothing could be done to end the bloodshed in Bosnia. They said, "Well, that's just the way those people in the Balkans are." But when we and our allies joined with courageous Bosnians to stand up to the aggressors, we helped to end the war. We learned that in the Balkans, inaction in the face of brutality simply invites more brutality, but firmness can stop armies and save lives. We must apply that lesson in Kosovo before what happened in Bosnia happens there, too.

Over the last few months we have done everything we possibly could to solve this problem peacefully. Secretary [of State Madeleine] Albright has worked tirelessly for a negotiated agreement. Mr. Milosevic has refused.

On Sunday I sent Ambassador Dick Holbrooke to Serbia to make clear to him again, on behalf of the United States and our NATO allies, that he must honor his own commitments and stop his repression, or face military action. Again, he refused.

Today we and our 18 NATO allies agreed to do what we said we would do, what we must do to restore the peace. Our mission is clear: to demonstrate the seriousness of NATO's purpose so that the Serbian leaders understand the imperative of reversing course; to deter an even bloodier offensive against innocent civilians in Kosovo and, if necessary, to seriously damage the Serbian military's capacity to harm the people of Kosovo. In short, if President Milosevic will not make peace, we will limit his ability to make war.

## A Forceful Response

Now, I want to be clear with you, there are risks in this military action, risks to our pilots and the people on the ground. Serbia's air defenses are strong. It could decide to intensify its assault on Kosovo or to seek to harm us or our allies elsewhere. If it does, we will deliver a forceful response.

Hopefully, Mr. Milosevic will realize his present course is self-destructive and unsustainable. If he decides to accept the peace agreement and demilitarize Kosovo, NATO has agreed to help to implement it with a peacekeeping force. If NATO is invited to do so, our troops should take part in that mission to keep the peace. But I do not intend to put our troops in Kosovo to fight a war.

Do our interests in Kosovo justify the dangers to our Armed Forces? I've thought long and hard about that question. I am convinced that the dangers of acting are far outweighed by the dangers of not acting—dangers to defenseless people and to our national interests. If we and our allies were to allow this war to continue with no response, President Milosevic would read our hesitation as a license to kill. There would be many more massacres, tens of thousands more refugees, more victims crying out for revenge.

Right now our firmness is the only hope the people of Kosovo have to be able to live in their own country without having to fear for their own lives. Remember: We asked them to accept peace, and they did. We asked them to promise to lay down their arms, and they agreed. We pledged that we, the United States and the

## President Clinton Announces the End of NATO Bombing in Kosovo

When I ordered our armed forces into combat, we had three clear goals: to enable the Kosovar people, the victims of some of the most vicious atrocities in Europe since the Second World War, to return to their homes with safety and self-government; to require Serbian forces responsible for those atrocities to leave Kosovo; and to deploy an international security force, with NATO at its core, to protect all the people of that troubled land, Serbs and Albanians alike.

Those goals will be achieved. Unnecessary conflict has been brought to a just and honorable conclusion.

The result will be security and dignity for the people of Kosovo, achieved by an alliance that stood together in purpose and resolve, assisted by the diplomatic efforts of Russia.

This victory brings a new hope that when a people are singled out for destruction because of their heritage and religious faith and we can do something about it, the world will not look the other way.

*Bill Clinton, "Text of President Clinton's Address to the Nation," New York Times, June 11, 1999. www.nytimes.com.*

other 18 nations of NATO, would stick by them if they did the right thing. We cannot let them down now.

Imagine what would happen if we and our allies instead decided just to look the other way, as these people were massacred on NATO's doorstep. That would discredit NATO, the cornerstone on which our security has rested for 50 years now.

We must also remember that this is a conflict with no natural national boundaries. . . . [The movement of refugees] is threatening the young democracy in Macedonia, which has its own Albanian minority and a Turkish minority. Already, Serbian forces have made forays into Albania from which Kosovars have drawn support. Albania has a Greek minority. Let a fire burn here in this area, and the flames will spread. Eventually, key U.S. allies could be drawn into a wider conflict, a war we would be forced to confront later, only at far greater risk and greater cost.

I have a responsibility as President to deal with problems such as this before they do permanent harm to our national interests. America has a responsibility to stand with our allies when they are trying to save innocent lives and preserve peace, freedom, and stability in Europe. That is what we are doing in Kosovo.

## A Secure Europe

If we've learned anything from the century drawing to a close, it is that if America is going to be prosperous and secure, we need a Europe that is prosperous, secure, undivided, and free. We need a Europe that is coming together, not falling apart, a Europe that shares our values and shares the burdens of leadership. That is the foundation on which the security of our children will depend.

That is why I have supported the political and economic unification of Europe. That is why we brought Poland, Hungary, and the Czech Republic into NATO, and redefined its missions,[2] and reached out to Russia and Ukraine for new partnerships.

Now, what are the challenges to that vision of a peaceful, secure, united, stable Europe?—the challenge of strengthening a partnership with a democratic Russia that, despite our disagreements, is a constructive partner in the work of building peace; the challenge of resolving the tension between Greece and Turkey and building bridges with the Islamic world; and finally, the challenge of ending instability in the Balkans so that these bitter ethnic problems in Europe are resolved by the force of argument, not the force of arms, so that future generations of Americans do not have to cross the Atlantic to fight another terrible war.

It is this challenge that we and our allies are facing in Kosovo. That is why we have acted now—because we care about saving innocent lives; because we have an interest in avoiding an even crueler and costlier war; and because our children need and deserve a peaceful, stable, free Europe.

Our thoughts and prayers tonight must be with the men and women of our Armed Forces who are undertaking this mission for the sake of our values and our children's future.

May God bless them, and may God bless America.

## Notes

1. The Cold War was the long period of tension between the United States and Communist Russia. It ended in the late 1980s when Russia's Communist government collapsed.
2. Before the end of the Cold War, NATO was mainly designed as an alliance to contain Communist Russia. After the fall of communism, it became focused on peacekeeping and security missions such as those in Kosovo.

# Serbs Committed Genocide and Gendercide in Kosovo

*Gendercide Watch*

*Gendercide Watch is an organization dedicated to confronting gender-selective mass killing around the world. In the following viewpoint, the organization argues that Serbians engaged in genocidal killing against Albanians in Kosovo. Gendercide Watch notes that before the Kosovo War, Serbs engaged in systematic discrimination against Albanians. The organization says that once the war began, genocidal actions were undertaken, especially against male Albanians. Gendercide Watch says that this amounted to gendercide, or a gender-specific atrocity. Gendercide Watch cites the testimony of survivors and forensic evidence from mass graves as evidence of gendercide and genocide.*

The genocidal assault launched against Kosovo's civilian population in 1998–99 bore many of the hallmarks of the earlier Serb campaigns in Bosnia [in the mid-1990s]. From a gender perspective, a strong trend was evident in the expulsion of women, children, and the elderly, the sexual assault of younger Kosovar women, and the systematic targeting of the "battle-age" male population for mass execution, detention, and torture. . . .

## The Background

The authoritarian Serb leader Slobodan Milosevic made Kosovo the cornerstone of his rise to power in 1987–89. As the Yugoslav federation disintegrated, Milosevic saw the opportunity to take control by inflaming nationalist sentiments, and eventually by "ethnically cleansing" territories where Serbs constituted a majority or a large minority. Kosovo was inflated in the Serb national consciousness as essential to the nation's identity. This clashed with the aspirations of the ethnic Albanians of Kosovo, some 90% of the population, who had enjoyed considerable autonomy within Marshal [Josip Broz] Tito's socialist federation [Communist Yugoslavia], and now watched as that autonomy was stripped away. In 1989, Milosevic arranged for Kosovo's "provincial" status within the Yugoslav federation to be cancelled, and closed down the provincial assembly and government. A police state was imposed, and ethnic Albanians were fired by the tens of thousands from state and private positions alike. These jobs now went to Serbs, and the migration, especially of young ethnic-Albanian men, was strongly "encouraged." Hundreds of thousands did indeed pour as refugees and economic migrants into Western Europe and North America, creating one of the largest diaspora communities in the world.

At street level, the pattern was one of constant surveillance, harassment, and detention of Kosovar men. Julie Mertus noted shortly before the outbreak of the war that "police routinely stop ethnic Albanian men"; she cites the astonishing statistic that between 1989 and 1997, "584,373 Kosovo Albanians—half the adult population—[was] arrested, interrogated, interned or remanded." Eventually, after nearly a decade of repression that many commentators have compared to South African apartheid,[1] an armed guerrilla movement (the Kosovo Liberation Army [KLA]) arose in 1997. The Milosevic regime seized the opportunity, and began to plan for an epic act of genocide and population transfer that would extinguish ethnic-Albanian culture in Kosovo once and for all.

As tension and violence increased in Kosovo over the course of 1998–99, there were signs that reprisal killings of males would be an essential Serb strategy in any full-scale conflict. The outbreak of mass killings in 1998 included a substantial number of women, elderly, and child victims—nearly always according to the variable of family affiliation. The assault on the Deliaj clan in September 1998, for example, left "the bodies of 15 women, children and elderly members" of the clan "slumped among the rocks and streams of the gorge below their village . . . shot in the head at close range and in some cases mutilated as they tried to escape advancing Serbian forces."

Among the cases of mutilation was that of a 30-year-old woman, Lumnije Deliaj, "who relatives said was seven months pregnant. Her abdomen had been slit open." Six more elderly people (at least four of them male) were shot or burned to death elsewhere in the village of Gornje Obrinje. But four miles away from this clan killing, at Golubovac, a mass murder was being carried out, with the victims selected according to a different and more typical standard. The gendercidal atrocity that ensued was related by one man, Selman Morina, who miraculously survived.

It was this pattern of gender-selective atrocity that again predominated prior to the outbreak of fullscale war. . . . The crowning prewar act of mass killing—depicted by some as "The massacre that forced the West to act"—occurred at the village of Racak on January 16, 1999. What happened was succinctly captured by Peter Beaumont and Patrick Wintour [in a 1999 *Guardian* article]: "As the [Serb] forces entered the village searching for 'terrorists' from the Kosovo Liberation Army, they tortured, humiliated, and murdered any men they found." . . . The international monitors who investigated the slaughter provided the most detailed accounting of the Racak victims:

*Chief of the Organization for Security and Co-operation in Europe mission in Kosovo, William Walker (center), looks at the bodies of dozens of dead men that were found on a hillside after the Racak massacre, which took place in January 1999. This massacre of ethnic Albanians by Serb forces made the international community take notice of the atrocities in Kosovo.* © AP Images/Visar Kryeziu.

Twenty-three adult males of various ages. Many shot at extremely close range, most shot in the front, back and top of the head. Villagers reported that these victims were last seen alive when the police were arresting them. . . . Three adults [*sic*] males shot in various parts of their body, including their backs. They appeared to have been shot when running away. . . . One adult male shot outside his house with his head missing. . . . One adult male shot in head and decapitated. All the flesh was missing from the skull. One adult female shot in the back. . . . One boy (12 years old) shot in the neck. One male, late teens (shot in abdomen). (Excerpts in the *New York Times*, January 22, 1999.)

After Racak, the international community, led by the United States, stepped up the pressure on the Milosevic regime, convening a conference at the French chateau of Rambouillet in an effort to strike a peace accord that would give Kosovo autonomy, though not fullscale independence, as the vast majority of ethnic Albanians were now demanding. The abortive negotiations at Rambouillet are one of the most hotly-debated aspects of the Kosovo war. . . . Regardless of the causes, the Serbs refused to sign the terms offered them, and withdrew to implement their "final solution" for the ethnic-Albanian "problem" in Kosovo—Operation Horseshoe.

## Operation Horseshoe

Operation Horseshoe was apparently the name given to the Serb offensive concentrated along, but not limited to, the semi-circular swath of western Kosovo adjoining Albania, which had been the heartland of KLA resistance. Beginning on March 19, 1999, and then escalating with the onset of NATO [North Atlantic Treaty Organization] airstrikes on Yugoslavia on March 24, the Serbs implemented a classic "ethnic cleansing" campaign focusing upon the expulsion of most of the population, the sexual assault of hundreds of Kosovar women, and above all the gender-selective mass execution of "battle-age" men who had been unable to escape to the hills or surrounding countries. Some of the first eyewitness testimony to the gendercide was brought to western attention by Selami Elshani, a Kosovar man who survived the massacre of more than 100 non-combatant men at the village of Velika Krusa on March 26, 1999. Severely burned by the fire the Serbs set to "finish off" their victims, Elshani was eventually smuggled across the border to Albania, where a *Washington Post* reporter interviewed him in his hospital bed.

Among the testimonials gathered by Human Rights Watch was that of a 20-year-old woman at Izbica, the site of another act of gendercide shortly after Velika Krusa. Her account made clear the ruthless gender-selectiveness that usually prevailed in the Serbs' "cleansing" campaigns:

> When the Serbs arrived, almost all of the young men left the village. They went into the mountains to hide or fight. . . . By 10 A.M. everyone was in the field. There were thousands of people, almost all women, children, and old people. Only about 150 men were among us. . . . At about 11 A.M. they separated the women from the men. We asked them why they were doing this and they told us, in a very scary voice: "Shut up, don't ask, otherwise we'll kill you." The children were terrified. The Serbs yelled: "We'll kill you, and where is the United States to save you?" All the women had covered their heads with handkerchiefs out of fear of [rape by] the Serbs, hiding their hair and foreheads. The Serbs called us obscene things, saying "F--- all Albanian mothers," and "All Albanian women are bitches." They took the men away and lined them up about twenty meters away from us. Then they ordered us to go to Albania. They said: "You've been looking for a greater Albania, now you can go there." They were shooting in the air above our heads. We followed their orders and moved in the direction we were told, walking away from the men. About 100 meters from the place we started walking, the Serbs decided to separate out the younger boys from our group. Boys of fourteen and up had already been placed with the men; now they separated out boys of about ten and up. Only very small boys were left with us, one old man who had lost his legs, and my handicapped brother, who can't walk because of spinal meningitis. So they took the ten-to-fourteen-year-olds to join the men. The boys' mothers were crying. Some even tried to speak to the Serbs, but the Serbs pushed them [away]. We were walking away very slowly because we were so worried about what would happen to our men.
>
> We stopped moving when we heard automatic weapon fire. We turned our heads to see what was happening, but it was impossible to see the men. We saw the ten-to-fourteen-year-olds running in our direction; when they got to us we

asked them what was happening. They were very upset; no one could talk. One of them finally told us: "They released us but the others are finished." We stayed in the same place for some twenty minutes. Everyone was crying. The automatic weapon fire went on non-stop for a few minutes; after that we heard short, irregular bursts of fire for some ten minutes or so. My father, my uncle and my cousin were among the men killed. Kajtaz Rexha and Qazim Rexhepi were also killed, as were many other members of the Bajraj, Bajrami, Rexhepi, and Aliu families. Then ten Serbs caught up with us. They said lots of obscenities and again told us: "Now you must leave for Albania—don't stop, just go." We had to leave. . . . My father had given me his jacket because I had been wearing another jacket that said "American Sport" on it and he was afraid; he wanted to cover that up. Because I was pushing the wheelbarrow and wearing a man's jacket, they thought I was a man. They told me to stop and then to come over to them, but I was too afraid. It was the scariest moment of my life. Then they shined a flashlight in my face and saw that I was a woman. One of them said, "Let her go." . . .

In the closing days of the war, grim and independently-sourced accounts circulated in British and U.S. newspapers of a Serb "factory of death" in Kosovo. It was alleged that the Serbs were using industrial sites such as the Trepca mines in northwestern Kosovo for the mass destruction and disposal of corpses. Perhaps the final gendercidal blast came at the Istok prison on May 20, where after a NATO airstrike, paramilitaries seized the opportunity to massacre over 100 ethnic-Albanian prisoners, all male.

## How Many Died?

The number of ethnic Albanians—and Serbs—killed during the Kosovo war is a matter of ongoing dispute, and solid estimates may not be possible for several years, if ever. The Kosovo war was unique in the history of international conflict, in that human-rights and forensics teams entered the territory on the heels of the arriving KFOR [NATO forces] troops. Between June and October 1999, the International Criminal Tribunal oversaw exhumations from some 175 graves of the 525 gravesites they said had been marked off for investigation. (How many might remain undiscovered, given the Tribunal's limited resources and Serb efforts to cover up the crimes, is not known.) Some two thousand bodies—2,108, to be precise—had been exhumed when the Tribunal issued its preliminary report in November 1999. Chief prosecutor Carla Del Ponte also spoke of widespread evidence of tampering with the gravesites and destruction of evidence—standard Serb procedure throughout the Balkans wars.

A striking statistic is that up to 10,000 Kosovars are registered with the authorities as missing—about the same number as in the entire Bosnian war, minus the massacres at Srebrenica;[2] and this is a war that is estimated to have killed 150–250,000 people. The death-toll in Kosovo is obviously much lower, in low five rather than low six figures. A reasonable speculation at this early stage is 20,000–30,000 killed and missing, of which the overwhelming majority are ethnic-Albanian civilians. No precise figures exist on the proportion of males among these casualties, but the outgoing chief prosecutor of the International Criminal Tribunal, Louise Arbour, has spoken of "conglomerations of military-age men" at the gravesites the Tribunal has exhumed, and it is fair to presume 90 percent or higher male dead. At some of the best-documented massacre sites—Meja, Izbica, Pusto Selo, Bela Crkva, Velika Krusa—the Serb killers took extraordinary measures to cover their tracks. In many cases, though investigators have bone fragments, items of clothing, spent rifle cartridges, video evidence, and satellite photographs to base their claims on, not to mention the overwhelming refugee testimony, there are few or no complete bodies to be found.

Allegations that the Serbs engaged in the mass destruction and disposal of bodies at the Trepca mines and other sites have not been confirmed. Although Tribunal spokespeople state that the matter remains under investigation, they say they have found "no solid evidence" of such operations. Gendercide Watch, while strongly supportive of the Tribunal's forensic and legal efforts, is critical of the lackadaisical and cursory character of the investigations conducted at Trepca and some other locations. . . . The Tribunal is scheduled to wind up its investigations late in 2000.

## Notes

1. Under apartheid, white South Africans oppressed the black majority.
2. The massacres at Srebrenica took place in July 1995 when eight thousand Bosnians were killed by Serb forces.

# Serbia Did Not Commit Genocide in Kosovo

*David N. Gibbs*

*David N. Gibbs is an associate professor of history and political science at the University of Arizona. In the following viewpoint, he argues that Serb actions in Kosovo did not rise to the level of genocide. On the contrary, he argues, before NATO airstrikes, the numbers of civilian deaths and refugees were relatively low in Kosovo compared to other counterinsurgency campaigns such as those launched by the United States in Vietnam in the 1960s and in Iraq in the 2000s. Gibbs also says that reported Serbian plans for genocide were exaggerated, and Serbian president Slobodan Milosevic was not the genocidal madman portrayed by the United States. Gibbs concludes that, given there was no genocide, the United States' case for humanitarian intervention in Kosovo was weak.*

Let us now consider . . . the argument that US and NATO [North Atlantic Treaty Organization] policy [in Kosovo] was motivated primarily by humanitarian considerations. [Serb leader Slobodan] Milošević, according to this view, was an aggressive and exceptionally warlike leader, a threat to the whole Balkan

David N. Gibbs, *First Do No Harm: Humanitarian Intervention and the Destruction of Yugoslavia*, Nashville, TN: Vanderbilt University Press, 2009, pp. 191–194. All rights reserved. Reproduced by permission.

region. With regard to Kosovo, "we're talking about the fourth war which Mr. Milošević ordered his forces to unleash," according to General [Klaus] Naumann [chairman of the NATO military committee]. It was also widely believed that Milošević was an irrational figure, "detached from reality," possibly due to psychiatric disturbances.[1] This interpretation argues that the United States was morally obligated to protect the Kosovar Albanians from violence and persecution, which were being directed by the Serb leader. The problem with such views is that they overstate Milošević's uglier characteristics; they exaggerate to an almost cartoonish extent. Milošević did not single-handedly trigger the previous wars in Slovenia, Croatia, and Bosnia-Herzegovina, as we have seen. Other leaders, such as Franjo Tudjman, played major roles in causing Yugoslavia's dissolution and the wars that followed. And we have no serious evidence that Milošević was acting irrationally.

## Humanitarianism and US Policy

In the case of Kosovo, both sides must bear responsibility for the upsurge in fighting. Even Tony Blair acknowledged (in private) that "the KLA [Kosovo Liberation Army] . . . were not much better than the Serbs." To argue that the Serbs alone were responsible is surely a distortion. And it is also a distortion to argue that Milošević was incapable of negotiating in good faith: He was perfectly capable of reaching agreements—and enforcing those agreements—when it was in his interest to do so. In Kosovo for example, he initially implemented the terms of the Holbrooke agreement[2] in the fall of 1998. The agreement broke down primarily because of *Albanian* attacks against Serbs, and this point is widely recognized. Overall, the allegation that Milošević was the sole cause of the fighting appears inconsistent with the record of events.

Yet another allegation was that Milošević had a long-standing scheme to expel virtually the entire Albanian population, and that NATO intervention was thus needed to protect the Albanians.

The main support for these claims was a revelation by German Defense Ministry officials that they had discovered a secret Serb plan, code-named Operation Horseshoe. This plan, supposedly crafted by the Serb military in 1998, called for the general removal of ethnic Albanians from Kosovo. The existence of this Serb plan was first widely reported in early April 1999 during the NATO air war, and it elicited extensive interest. Critically, it was emphasized that Horseshoe was not a contingency plan, but a firm intention to expel the Albanians; it was to be implemented whether or not NATO commenced bombing.

In fact, the Horseshoe allegations were based on very thin evidence, and it now seems doubtful that such a plan ever existed. After the war was over, German brigadier general Heinz Loquai revealed that the whole operation was "fabricated from run-of-the-mill Bulgarian intelligence reports." General Loquai claimed that German officials "turned a vague report from Sofia into a 'plan,' and even coined the name Horseshoe." Loquai also noted that German officials had misrepresented the contents of the Bulgarian reports, which actually emphasized Serb plans to destroy the KLA, not the Albanian population more generally. When considered in retrospect, Operation Horseshoe looks like fairly standard wartime propaganda.

And finally, it was widely alleged that the Serbs had committed genocide in Kosovo. In a public speech on March 23, 1999, President [Bill] Clinton cited the genocide argument as one of his main justifications for the 1999 NATO war. Since the end of the war, however, this claim also has lost credibility. In fact, international tribunals (quietly) determined that the Kosovo atrocities did *not* qualify as genocide. At the International Criminal Tribunal for the Former Yugoslavia, for example, none of the three separate indictments against Milošević mentioned the crime of genocide with respect to Kosovo. In each of the three documents of indictment, Milošević was accused of committing various crimes in Kosovo—but the word "genocide" appeared nowhere. Apparently, the case for genocide was sufficiently weak

## Franjo Tudjman

Slobodan Milosevic, the president of Serbia, is widely associated with acts of ethnic cleansing and genocide within the former Yugoslavia during the 1990s. However, he is not the only figure who has been accused of atrocities. Another widely reviled leader of the period is Franjo Tudjman.

Tudjman was a historian, writer, and politician who became the first president of Croatia in 1990. He quickly moved to consolidate autocratic power, shutting down newspapers that disagreed with him and promoting members of his own family into positions of authority.

Tudjman was an avowed racist, who spoke of his admiration for the Nazis and referred to Bosnian Muslims as "dirty stinking Asians." Tudjman's Croatia built concentration camps and engaged in ethnic cleansing during the Bosnian conflict of the early 1990s, forcing Muslims out of areas inhabited by Croats. Tudjman moved to eliminate the traditional protections afforded to Serbs in Croatia, resulting in a Serb uprising. Tudjman succeeded in suppressing the uprising in 1995. A massive exodus of Serbs resulted.

Tudjman was never tried for war crimes, in part because he maintained better relations with the West than Milosevic did. He died in 1999.

that not even the prosecution wished to pursue the matter. And in a separate 2001 case, the UN-directed Supreme Court of Kosovo concluded that Serb atrocities "were not genocide."

## Serb Atrocities in Perspective

It is of course indisputable that Serb forces committed atrocious acts in Kosovo—including systematic attacks against civilians who sympathized with the KLA—and that these attacks occurred both before and after the NATO bombing. Even if we leave aside the provocative accusation that Serb crimes amounted to genocide, the crimes that *did* occur were terrible enough. At the

Milošević trial, Lord [Paddy] Ashdown emphasized the Serbs' "excessive, outrageous" use of force during counterinsurgency sweeps. There is no doubt that the Serbs used excessive force in Kosovo, and such actions deserve condemnation.

As a justification for Western intervention, however, the "excessive force" argument seems questionable. Compared with other counterinsurgency wars, the Serb actions in Kosovo were relatively mild. During the period up to the start of the NATO air war, the total number of deaths on both sides (both military and civilian) was two thousand. The number of Albanian civilians killed by Serb forces has never been estimated precisely, but it was probably in the range of several hundred. This surely is a ghastly figure, but it is *not* large for a counterinsurgency war. Charges of mass murder, at least during this phase, were greatly overstated. In Kosovo, there also was a substantial number of refugees generated by the fighting, which totaled about 200,000 by March 1999. But refugee flows are common during counterinsurgencies, including several conducted by members of the Contact Group that organized the Rambouillet conference [a 1999 peace conference]. If one considers the US war in Vietnam, the French in Algeria, the British in Kenya, the Russians in Afghanistan—or even the recent [2003–2011] US-led counterinsurgency in Iraq—the Kosovo case does not stand out for its atrocities. When compared with other wars, the Serb methods of counterinsurgency do not seem unusually cruel or extreme.

## Comparing Counterinsurgencies

To gain some historical perspective, let us consider a more detailed comparison. The case I have chosen for comparison is a counterinsurgency campaign conducted on Cheju Island in South Korea during 1948–1949. The Cheju case involved an uprising by a left-wing People's Army that was repressed by central government security forces and their associated militias. Cheju Island had some features in common with Kosovo and is thus a useful comparison case. As in Kosovo, in the Cheju rebellion the insurgents had overwhelming support from the local inhabitants, who opposed the central government. The duration of the fighting in Cheju—more than a year at its peak—was comparable to that of the war in Kosovo. Cheju was a small and geographically isolated area; with only about 250,000 people, it was much less populated than Kosovo. Regarding the extent of killings in Cheju during the counterinsurgency, Bruce Cumings provides this account: "American sources estimate that 15,000 to 20,000 islanders died, but the ROK [South Korean government] official figure was 27,719. The North said that more than 30,000 islanders had been 'butchered' in the suppression. The governor of Cheju, however, privately told American intelligence that 60,000 had died. . . . In other words, one in every five or six islanders had perished." This description of the Cheju case gives some sense of what a truly unrestrained counterinsurgency against a relatively small population looks like. The brutality in Kosovo did not reach this level, or anything close to it. The exceptional attention paid to the atrocities in Kosovo must be considered, at least in part, a result of media sensationalism and governmental exaggeration.

Overall, the argument in favor of a humanitarian motivation for US policy is unpersuasive. As we have seen, the United States supported the Kosovo Liberation Army, despite its unsavory record. And when the KLA sought to undermine the Holbrooke agreement, and did so with success, the United States declined to restrain the guerrillas. Indeed, the United States began providing direct military aid to the KLA, thus rewarding the guerrillas for triggering an upsurge in fighting. At Rambouillet, the United States took actions that virtually guaranteed a collapse of the peace talks and made war inevitable. According to [British politician] Lord [John] Gilbert, such actions were taken deliberately, with the intent of scuttling the peace talks. The US insistence on using war as a solution to ethnic conflict in Kosovo—well before it had exhausted possible diplomatic solutions—seems inconsistent with a humanitarian intent.

_Kosovo_

## Notes

1. According to an anonymous US official.
2. Named for US diplomat Richard Holbrooke, this agreement ended the Bosnian war.

# Serbians Used Rape as an Instrument of Ethnic Cleansing Against Albanians in Kosovo

*Human Rights Watch*

*Human Rights Watch (HRW) is an international human rights organization. In the following viewpoint, the organization reports that it documented ninety-six incidents of rape by Serbian forces against Albanians. HRW believes that many more rapes were committed by Serb forces during the conflict than were reported. It says that these rapes were part of a deliberate effort to terrorize the Albanian population and force them to flee Kosovo. HRW adds that Serb officials knew about the rapes but did nothing to prevent them or to bring the perpetrators to justice. The authors conclude that international authorities should investigate and prosecute the rapes as war crimes.*

On the evening of March 24, 1999, the North Atlantic Treaty Organization (NATO) began bombing the Federal Republic of Yugoslavia. As Serbian police and Yugoslav Army forces continued brutal attacks on civilians, more than 800,000 ethnic Albanian refugees poured out of Kosovo, mostly into Albania and Macedonia. Exhausted and traumatized, they carried what few belongings they could grab before fleeing or being expelled. They also brought eyewitness accounts of atrocities committed against ethnic Albanian civilians inside Kosovo by Yugoslav soldiers, Serbian police, and paramilitaries.

## Rape as a Weapon of War

Witnesses and victims told of summary executions, mass murders, destruction of civilian property, and other war crimes. In more hushed tones, refugees also spoke of rapes of ethnic Albanian women. These instances of sexual violence are the focus of this report.

Human Rights Watch began investigating the use of rape and other forms of sexual violence by all sides in the conflict in 1998 and continued to document rape accounts throughout the refugee crisis in 1999. After NATO troops entered Kosovo in June 1999, Human Rights Watch returned to Kosovo to continue researching war crimes, including the use of sexual violence before, during, and after the NATO conflict. In total, Human Rights Watch researchers conducted approximately seven hundred interviews between March and September 1999 on various violations of international humanitarian law.

The research found that rape and other forms of sexual violence were used in Kosovo in 1999 as weapons of war and instruments of systematic "ethnic cleansing." Rapes were not rare and isolated acts committed by individual Serbian or Yugoslav forces, but rather were used deliberately as an instrument to terrorize the civilian population, extort money from families, and push people to flee their homes. Rape furthered the goal of forcing ethnic Albanians from Kosovo.

In total, Human Rights Watch found credible accounts of ninety-six cases of sexual assault by Yugoslav soldiers, Serbian police, or paramilitaries during the period of NATO bombing, and the actual number is probably much higher. In six of these cases, Human Rights Watch was able to interview the victims in depth, and their testimonies are contained in this report. Human

Rights Watch met two other women who acknowledged that they had been raped but refused to give testimony. And, Human Rights Watch documented six cases of women who were raped and subsequently killed.

The ninety-six cases also include rape reports deemed reliable by Human Rights Watch that were compiled by other nongovernmental organizations. The Center for the Protection of Women and Children, based in Pristina (Prishtina) [the capital of Kosovo], interviewed and provided assistance to twenty-nine rape and sexual violence victims after June 1999. The Albanian Counseling Center for Women and Girls, an NGO [nongovernmental organization] in Albania, documented an additional twenty-eight rape cases through direct interviews with victims. The Yugoslavia-based Humanitarian Law Center provided testimony to Human Rights Watch about four cases. And the Council for the Defense of Human Rights and Freedoms, Kosovo's largest human rights group, provided information on an additional four cases. To the extent possible, Human Rights Watch corroborated these accounts through interviews with dozens of nurses, doctors, eyewitnesses, and local human rights and women's rights activists.

Médécins Sans Frontières (MSF [also known as Doctors Without Borders]), with offices in Kosovo before and after the war, reported four cases of rape, and other medical personnel working in Kosovo and Albania confirmed an additional eight cases. Physicians for Human Rights, a U.S.-based human rights group, interviewed four victims of sexual violence, and Amnesty International documented another three cases of rape, although two of these three cases were also counted by Human Rights Watch.

It is important to note that some of these cases may have been double-counted by local and international organizations. Despite this, Human Rights Watch believes that the actual number of women raped in Kosovo between March and June 1999 was much higher than ninety-six. Kosovar Albanian victims of

*Human Rights Watch workers went to the city of Pec (pictured) and other villages to interview victims and witnesses of sexual assault during the Kosovo War.* © AP Images/Lefteris Pitarakis.

rape are generally reluctant to speak about their experiences, and those who remained in Kosovo throughout the conflict may not have had an opportunity to report abuses. At the same time, it should be noted that Human Rights Watch was not able to confirm the allegations of rape camps in Kosovo that were presented during the war by the U.S. and British governments, as well as by NATO.

## Sanctioned Rapes

In general, rapes in Kosovo can be grouped into three categories: rapes in women's homes, rapes during flight, and rapes in detention. In the first category, security forces entered private homes and raped women either in the yard, in front of family members, or in an adjoining room. In the second category, internally displaced people wandering on foot and riding on tractors were repeatedly stopped, robbed, and threatened by the Yugoslav Army, Serbian police, or paramilitaries. If families could not produce cash, security forces told them that their daughters would be taken away and raped; in some cases, even when families did provide money, their daughters were taken away. The third category of rapes took place in temporary detention centers, such as abandoned homes or barns.

With few exceptions, the rapes here documented by Human Rights Watch were gang rapes involving at least two perpetrators. In several cases, victims and witnesses identified the perpetrators as Serbian special police, in blue or blue-camouflage uniforms, or Yugoslav Army soldiers, in green military uniforms. The majority of rape cases, however, were evidently committed by Serbian paramilitaries, who wore various uniforms and often had bandanas, long knives, long hair, and beards. These paramilitary formations worked closely with official government forces, either the Serbian Ministry of Interior or the Yugoslav Army, throughout Kosovo.

The Serbian and Yugoslav authorities knew that their paramilitaries had used rape and other forms of sexual violence in Bosnia and Herzegovina. Yet, the paramilitaries were deployed to or allowed to operate in Kosovo by the Serbian and Yugoslav authorities apparently without any precautions being taken to prevent their committing further such war crimes.

The participation of Serbian and Yugoslav forces in gang rapes renders it unlikely that senior officers were unaware of the assaults. Rapes occurred frequently in the presence, and with the acquiescence, of military officers. Several rape victims actually reported the crimes to Yugoslav military officers. Yet there is no evidence that the Yugoslav Army or the Serbian Ministry of Interior made any attempt to apprehend or punish those responsible for the attacks. Despite this seeming dereliction of duty, many leading police and military officers from the Kosovo campaign have been honored or promoted within the Serbian and Yugoslav forces since the end of the conflict.

There is also no evidence that the Yugoslav Army or Serbian Ministry of Interior took any measures to prevent rape and other forms of sexual violence, such as issuing orders or warning troops that they would be punished for these crimes. Moreover, soldiers, police, and paramilitaries often raped in front of many witnesses. In addition to actual rapes that took place in front of others, the process of pulling women out of refugee convoys often occurred in full view of other internally displaced persons (IDPs).

## Rape Should Be Prosecuted

Although the terror of imminent and actual violence is behind Kosovar Albanian women, many now face its devastating consequences and a struggle for justice. Kosovar women sexually assaulted or raped by Yugoslav soldiers, Serbian paramilitaries, and police have suffered war crimes, torture, and some abuses that may have constituted crimes against humanity. The international community must now respond by seeking to identify and by indicting those responsible for these violations of humanitarian law. Without serious investigations of rape and sexual violence, and indictments and arrests of those with command responsibility and individual responsibility for these crimes, rape in the region will continue with impunity. Kosovar Albanian women are waiting for justice.

The International Criminal Tribunal for the Former Yugoslavia (ICTY) has jurisdiction over the crimes committed in Kosovo. ICTY Prosecutor Carla Del Ponte has outlined a prosecution strategy that "focuses on leadership investigative targets, as well as perpetrators of particularly serious crimes or sexual violence in relation to the armed conflict." The Office of the Prosecutor issued indictments against Serbian leader Slobodan Milosevic and three other top Serbian leaders and a general in the Yugoslav Army on May 24, 1999, for crimes against humanity. Not one of the indictments lists charges relating to the use of rape and other forms of sexual violence by their forces, although the investigations are ongoing.

Since the entry of the NATO-led Kosovo Force (KFOR), rapes of Serbian, Albanian, and Roma women by ethnic Albanians, sometimes by members of the Kosovo Liberation Army (KLA), have also been documented. Human Rights Watch condemns these human rights violations and continues to document post-conflict abuses for a future report. However, rapes and other crimes of sexual violence committed since the entry of KFOR are beyond the scope of this report.

Specifically to investigate rape, Human Rights Watch visited the cities of Pec (Peje), Djakovica (Gjakove), Podujevo (Podujeve), Mitrovica (Mitrovice), Decani (Decane), Vucitrn (Vushtrri), and Pristina, as well as many other villages throughout Kosovo. Human Rights Watch interviewed rape and sexual assault victims, witnesses to sexual violence, medical personnel, representatives of nongovernmental organizations, United Nations officials, Organization for Security and Cooperation in Europe (OSCE) experts, and human rights activists in Kosovo and Albania. Human Rights Watch drew its findings on rape and sexual violence from interviews with victims and eyewitnesses and the credible reports of human rights and other service organizations. Whenever possible, Human Rights Watch collected several accounts of the same event for purposes of corroboration.

# Albanians Have Committed Ethnic Cleansing Against Roma People in Kosovo

*Sani Rifati*

*Sani Rifati is a Romani activist, writer, and lecturer from Kosovo. He is the president of Voice of Roma, a nonprofit organization working on behalf of Roma (sometimes referred to as Gypsies) in Kosovo. In the following viewpoint, he reports that Roma in Kosovo face ongoing hardship and discrimination. The Roma, he says, have been forced from their homes in an act of deliberate ethnic cleansing by Albanians, who are the majority ethnic group in Kosovo. He says that Roma now live in internally displaced person camps (IDPs) in severe poverty. International forces that were supposed to ensure human rights in Kosovo have been uninterested in helping the Roma—probably, Rifati says, because of longstanding European prejudices against Roma people.*

I am a Rom (more commonly known as "Gypsy") who was born in Kosovo, Yugoslavia, and lived in Pristina (the capital of the Kosovo region) for 27 years. In the summer of 2000, ten years later, I was only 30 miles away in Macedonia but I could not visit the town where I lived most of my life. This was more than three years after the "humanitarian bombing" by U.S.-NATO forces and escalation of ethnic conflict began in Kosovo on March 24th, 1999. But it was still too dangerous for me, as a dark-skinned "Madjupi" (Albanian term connoting "lower than garbage"), to set foot inside of Kosovo.

## Home Wiped Away

Finally, the day arrived (May 2nd, 2002) when I could visit my place of birth, the place of so many memories from my youth. But that place—where I grew up with my four brothers and one sister, cousins, relatives, neighbors, friends—no longer existed. Everything had been wiped away. The new and renovated houses, villas, gas stations, motels, all built in the past three years by the triumphant ethnic Albanians, made Kosovo look like a foreign country to me. I didn't know what to feel in that moment of returning. Fear, happiness, anger, sadness?

The paradox that crossed my mind was that all this rebuilding is being sponsored by international relief agencies and financed by development and investment companies with such well-known heads as [former US vice president] Dick Cheney and George Soros [a well-known businessman]. Meanwhile the Roma, Serbs, Gorani, Bosnians, Turks and other minorities in Kosovo are starving! While most of these international institutions were bragging about "free and democratic Kosovo," these peoples were forced to abandon their homes, suffering a "humanitarian" supported ethnic cleansing that has been virtually invisible to the rest of the world. The ironic consequence of NATO/U.S. rescue of oppressed Albanians is that they then became oppressors themselves.

This May [2002], as President of Voice of Roma (VOR), I led a trip to Kosovo with delegates representing human rights, refugee assistance, and peace groups from the U.S., Germany, Italy, and Holland. Most people working in such organizations think that Kosovo is free now, and that its people are living in harmony and peace. They are surprised when I inform them that the ethnic minorities in Kosovo are still fleeing. I wanted them to witness with their own eyes what is going on there.

The delegates were housed in the Romani communities, south of Pristina. Each family hosted two or more delegates. The delegates spent time with and got to know people who had been caught in heavy crossfire between Serbs and Albanians, suffered from the heavy bombing by NATO's U.S.-led forces, and experienced discrimination by K-FOR forces [NATO forces in Kosovo], the U.N. Police, international non-governmental organizations (NGOs), and Western European foreign policies. The delegates were appalled by the stories they heard and shocked at the conditions under which the Kosovo Roma were living.

## Ethnic Cleansing Goes On

Since NATO's "peace-keepers" arrived in Kosovo, more than 300,000 ethnic minorities have been "cleansed" from the region by extremist Albanians. It has been more than a year since the U.N. Interim Administration Mission in Kosovo (UNMIK) or the Organization for Security and Cooperation in Europe (OSCE) released any statements about human rights abuses of minorities in Kosovo. Surprisingly, such NGOs as Doctors Without Borders (winner of the Nobel Peace Prize), the International Red Cross, Oxfam, and many more have failed the ethnic minorities in Kosovo by not addressing their problems. Amnesty International and Human Rights Watch are alone in reporting on minority human rights abuses in Kosovo.

My question is: If NATO's so-called humanitarian bombing was to stop "ethnic cleansing," why are the same Western powers now so unwilling to intervene on behalf of the actual ethnic cleansing of Romani people and other minorities in Kosovo?

The ethnic cleansing of the Roma since U.N. peace-keepers arrived in June 12th of 1999 has resulted in more than 75% of this population (over 100,000 Romani people) fleeing Kosovo. Still the media and the international "humanitarian" community are silent. U.S. and Western media did not catch any of these

*Roma refugees forced to leave their homes during the Kosovo War live in camps near toxic waste, in extremely poor conditions, and with no running water.* © Carsten Koall/Getty Images News/Getty Images.

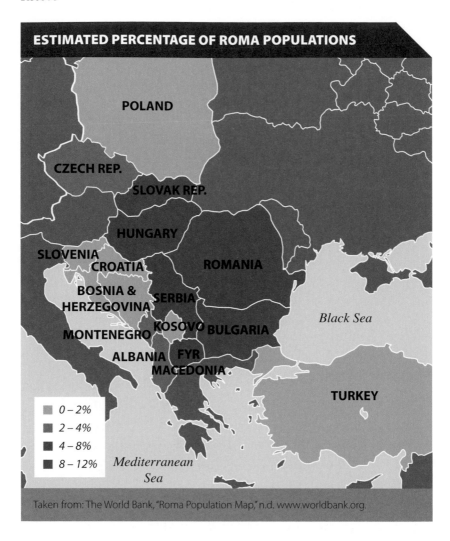

**ESTIMATED PERCENTAGE OF ROMA POPULATIONS**

POLAND

CZECH REP.

SLOVAK REP.

HUNGARY

SLOVENIA
CROATIA

ROMANIA

BOSNIA &
HERZEGOVINA   SERBIA

Black Sea

MONTENEGRO   KOSOVO   BULGARIA

ALBANIA   FYR
MACEDONIA

TURKEY

- 0 – 2%
- 2 – 4%
- 4 – 8%
- 8 – 12%

*Mediterranean
Sea*

Taken from: The World Bank, "Roma Population Map," n.d. www.worldbank.org.

events on their radar screens, or rather willingly ignored these
horrors.

The majority of the Roma who are left in Kosovo (25,000 out
of a prewar population of 150,000) are internal refugees, but they
do not have the official status of refugees. Instead these Roma are
labeled "internally-displaced persons" (IDPs), with fewer recognized rights than refugees, and are restricted to camps with
very poor facilities. Some Roma do live in Serbian controlled en-
claves. No other ethnic group is in the IDP camps, only Roma.

Why is this? Only the Roma have no safe haven country. Serbs flee to Serbia, Bosnians to Bosnia, Turks to Turkey, and Gorani (who are Muslim/Slavs) to Macedonia or Western Europe.

## Poverty and Oppression

The poorest of the poor, in the IDP camps, the Roma face a remarkable level of discrimination and oppression that is threatening their lives and crippling their culture. Just to give you an idea, the U.N. provides to each of the Roma in IDP camps a monthly ration of eight kilos (17 pounds) of flour, two onions, two tomatoes, a half-kilo (one pound) of cheese, and some fruit (usually rotten). Beyond that, there is only three liters of cooking oil per family, regardless of family size; no other supplies are available (interviews with refugees in IDP camps in Kosovo and Macedonia). If these people are struggling to survive physically, what then happens to their culture?

For another example, when a U.N. representative was approached by a VOR representative about providing cooking and drinking water to Roma in one camp, his reply was, "Oh, the Gypsies know how to take care of themselves. They're nomads; they've lived all their lives like that." If the Roma are facing such dismissal from those on whom they depend for their physical survival, how are they to survive either physically or culturally?

This deeply-rooted stereotype, that the Roma are uncivilized wanderers who don't have the same needs as members of "civilized" societies, is contradicted by the facts. In Kosovo, Roma have lived in houses for over seven hundred years, and most of them have never seen a wanderer's caravan. The effect of such stereotypes is to dehumanize the Roma and destroy their cultural infrastructure.

In today's "free" Kosovo, no Rom can move freely; his children cannot go to school, and cannot speak their mother tongue. Because they had to leave their homes and now must stay in the camps, most of the Roma still in Kosovo have not seen nearby family members in more than three years. That means, among other things, that marriages cannot be made according to Romani social rules. What happens to a society in which new families cannot form?

How can we change the situation of Roma, wherever they may happen to be? What is our responsibility to a people who have been so abused and ignored for centuries?

# The NATO Air Campaign in Serbia Was Just and Necessary

## George Robertson

*George Robertson, also known as Lord Robertson of Port Ellen, was the tenth Secretary General of NATO, the North Atlantic Treaty Organization. In the following viewpoint, he argues that the 1999 NATO airstrike on Serbia was just, necessary, and successful. He argues that NATO worked hard to keep civilian casualties to a minimum and was largely successful in achieving that goal. He says that NATO was justified in its actions even without a specific UN mandate. He argues that Serbian forces were intent on committing mass violence against Albanians, and the NATO air campaign was necessary to prevent ethnic cleansing and violence. He concludes that the NATO action prevented the kind of mass tragedy that occurred a few years earlier in the Balkan war in Bosnia.*

The concept for *Operation Allied Force* [the NATO campaign against Serbia] envisaged a phased air campaign, designed to achieve NATO's [North Atlantic Treaty Organization] political objectives with minimum force. The phases ranged from a show of force in the initial stages, to operations against Serb forces in Kosovo, expanding if necessary to targets throughout the Federal Republic of Yugoslavia that supported the regime's ability to attack the civilian population of Kosovo. It had been hoped, but never assumed, that [Serbian] President [Slobodan] Milosevic would quickly realise NATO's determination, and accept its demands. Instead, his campaign of ethnic cleansing escalated and, in response, NATO's leadership accelerated and strengthened its air campaign considerably.

## Selecting Targets

The air campaign set out to weaken Serb military capabilities, both strategically and tactically. Strikes on tactical targets, such as artillery and field headquarters, had a more immediate effect in disrupting the ethnic cleansing of Kosovo. Strikes against strategic targets, such as government ministries and refineries, had a longer-term and broader impact on the Serb military machine. Just over 38,000 combat sorties, including 10,484 strike sorties, were flown by Allied forces, with no Allied combat fatalities—a remarkable achievement.

Initially, it was vital to defeat the Serb air defence network. This proved a tough challenge, as it was highly developed and had many mobile elements. But without air superiority, NATO would not have been able effectively to achieve its military objectives while protecting its own forces, and the ability of Allied forces to strike military targets precisely and minimise "collateral damage" would have been reduced. While NATO successfully suppressed the threat, it was never eliminated, requiring constant vigilance throughout the campaign.

The bulk of NATO's effort against tactical targets was aimed at military facilities, fielded forces, heavy weapons, and military vehicles and formations in Kosovo and southern Serbia. Many of these targets were highly mobile and hard to locate, especially during the poor weather of the early phase of the campaign. Strikes were also complicated by the cynical Serb use of civilian homes and buildings to hide weapons and vehicles, the intermixing of military vehicles with civilian convoys and, sometimes, the use of human shields. In this way, NATO's concern to avoid civilian casualties was exploited by the Serbs. But the constant presence of NATO aircraft inhibited the Serbs by forcing them into hiding and frequently punishing them when they did venture out.

Strategic targets included Serb air defences, command and control facilities, Yugoslav military (VJ) and police (MUP) forces headquarters, and supply routes. NATO was sometimes criticised for such strikes, by those who said NATO's actions also risked both civilians and civilian property. In fact, the Alliance carefully selected targets based on their role in the Serb war effort. Facilities were only attacked when it was assessed that they made an effective contribution to the Yugoslav military effort and that their destruction offered a definite military advantage. Massive effort was made to minimise the impact of the air campaign on the Serb civilian population.

## Minimizing the Risk to Civilians

The selection of targets was carefully reviewed at multiple levels of command, as well as by the Allies carrying out the strikes. These reviews ensured they complied with international law, were militarily justified, and minimised the risk to civilian lives and property.

In fact, the concern to avoid unintentional damage was a principal constraining factor throughout. Many targets were not attacked because the risk to non-combatants was considered too high. But such restrictions did not alter the ultimate outcome. Modern technology, the skill of NATO's pilots, and control over target selection made it possible for the Alliance to succeed with remarkably few civilian casualties.

The actual toll in human lives will never be precisely known, but the independent group, Human Rights Watch, has estimated that there were 90 incidents involving civilian deaths, in which between 488 and 527 civilians may have lost their lives—87 of

*Albanians greet NATO troops as they enter Kosovo in June 1999.* © Ami Vitale/Getty Images News/Getty Images.

these at Korisa, where the Serb forces forced civilians to occupy a known military target. These figures are far lower than the 1,200–5,700 civilian deaths claimed by the Yugoslavs.

NATO deeply regrets any civilian casualties it caused, but these losses must be viewed in perspective against what NATO was seeking to prevent, and the actions of the Belgrade regime. Any historical study shows that Alliance aircrew set and achieved remarkably high standards. It is unrealistic to expect all risk to be eliminated. This is something that was well understood and was frequently stated openly by Kosovar Albanians themselves.

Despite cynical Serb attempts to exploit images of accidental civilian casualties from NATO air strikes, the Alliance held firm. President Milosevic calculated that if he held on long enough, it would weaken. He was wrong. The length of the air campaign did put stress on the Allies, but the unity and common purpose that lies at the core of NATO was equal to it. The steady increase in Allied airpower and effectiveness, and the realisation that NATO was holding together, played a fundamental part in the Serb climb-down. . . .

## A Just and Necessary Action

The abuse of human rights by the government of the Federal Republic of Yugoslavia, and the humanitarian disaster which NATO's intervention in Kosovo reversed, threatened to undermine the values on which the new Europe is being built. The Yugoslav regime's barbaric actions raised the spectre of instability spilling over to neighbouring countries, including derailing the peace process in Bosnia and Herzegovina.[1] If NATO had failed to respond to the policy of ethnic cleansing, it would have betrayed its values and cast permanent doubt on the credibility of its institutions. By facing up to President Milosevic's challenge, NATO nations confirmed that common values and respect for human rights are central to the Alliance and all the world's democracies.

NATO's success has not blinded the Alliance to the need to learn lessons from the conflict, and that process is continuing. The Kosovo campaign revealed gaps in NATO's military capabilities, especially in Europe, which need to be overcome. NATO is already acting through the Defence Capabilities Initiative (DCI) and through strengthening the European "pillar" of NATO by developing the European Security and Defence Identity (ESDI). NATO nations are already addressing these shortfalls. The challenge is to reorganise and re-equip our forces to make them more flexible, more mobile and more effective, and the need to do so is urgent. We cannot know when or where the next crisis will occur. The necessary resources must be provided.

Nevertheless, the air campaign achieved its goals in less than three months, with remarkably few civilian casualties, and no NATO combat casualties. The coalition held together and all states neighbouring the Federal Republic of Yugoslavia supported NATO's actions, despite the political and economic risks to their own countries. NATO will not forget this support. Nor will it forget the particular role played by Partnership for Peace nations, who were both steadfast and instrumental in achieving success, during the crisis and in its aftermath. Support for KFOR [NATO forces in Kosovo] is widespread and today, there are 19 non-NATO nations actively participating in KFOR peacekeeping, including Russia, which is a key partner in keeping and maintaining a permanent peace.

NATO understands the fundamental importance of long-term success in the Balkans. It will not be easy. No-one should expect dramatic improvements overnight. Much has been done, and much remains to be done. NATO will remain firm in its resolve to pursue the humanitarian and democratic objectives we all share.

## Assessing the Conduct of the Operation

It is a strength of our democracies that even when a military operation is successful and commands overwhelming international support, many will question whether it should have been undertaken—on policy or legal grounds—and, once undertaken, whether it should have been conducted differently. A year on, it is worth reviewing such criticism to try to present the issues fairly. . . .

*Were NATO's actions legally justified without a mandate from the UN Security Council?*

Some argue that NATO should not have acted against the Federal Republic of Yugoslavia in Kosovo without a specific United Nations Security Council mandate. The Allies were sensitive to the legal basis for their action. The Yugoslavs had already failed to comply with numerous demands from the Security Council under Chapter VII of the UN Charter and there was a major discussion in the North Atlantic Council, during which the Council took the following factors into consideration:

- the Yugoslav government's non-compliance with earlier UN Security Council resolutions,

- the warnings from the UN Secretary General about the dangers of a humanitarian disaster in Kosovo,
- the risk of such a catastrophe in the light of Yugoslavia's failure to seek a peaceful resolution of the crisis,
- the unlikelihood that a further UN Security Council resolution would be passed in the near future,
- and the threat to peace and security in the region.

At that point, the Council agreed that a sufficient legal basis existed for the Alliance to threaten and, if necessary, use force against the Federal Republic of Yugoslavia.

Had NATO not acted, the Yugoslav regime would have continued its brutal repression of the Albanian population of Kosovo. Today those who survived the ethnic savagery and the ravages of the winter would still be living in refugee camps outside their country, and the region would have been condemned to continuing warfare and instability for years to come. . . .

*Was NATO's bombing campaign poorly conceived and executed?*
Some argue that NATO's air campaign should have been more aggressive, striking at the heart of power in Belgrade at an earlier stage, while others have criticised NATO's decision not to deploy ground troops for an invasion of Kosovo.

Such a debate is theoretical—NATO won with the strategy it used. Airpower worked. We must not forget that NATO decided to employ military force to achieve limited political objectives—to end the violence and repression—not to militarily defeat Yugoslavia. As mentioned elsewhere, President Milosevic's only hope was to divide the Alliance, so any NATO strategy had to preserve Alliance unity and to reflect the democratic wishes of all 19 nations. Avoiding unnecessary suffering among the Serb population was also vital in maintaining public and international support for NATO's actions.

As the Serb repression in Kosovo accelerated, NATO responded quickly to intensify the air campaign. And as the air

## TARGETING COMMAND, CONTROL, AND COMMUNICATIONS

○ Areas of radio and TV outage

■ Command and control targets

▲ Communications

Paralyzing communications was a top priority. This chart details areas where air attacks knocked out and degraded radio and TV coverage. About 45% of the TV broadcast capability was degraded and a third of the military and civilian radio relay networks were damaged.

Source: Air Force Association, "Targeting Command, Control, and Communications," *The Kosovo Campaign: Airpower Made It Work*, 2011. www.afa.org/media/reports/campaign.asp. Copyright © 2011 by Air Force Association. All rights reserved. Reproduced by permission.

campaign lengthened other military options were seriously discussed at NATO and in national capitals. Nations were understandably reluctant to launch a ground invasion, which would have been time-consuming, difficult and expensive, in terms of lives as well as money and equipment. Nevertheless, many believe that NATO would have taken this step if necessary. It is probable that President Milosevic came to believe that we would do so, if necessary, and this may have been one of the reasons for his capitulation. . . .

*Did NATO's air campaign itself cause the ethnic cleansing it intended to stop?*

Some claim the brutal ethnic cleansing, violence and refugee exodus was precipitated by NATO's air campaign. The facts do not support this. President Milosevic's ethnic cleansing in Kosovo was well prepared and rehearsed. . . . It was preceded by a military build-up that was underway even as the Rambouillet [peace] talks were in progress. Later intelligence showed that he had a pre-planned strategy (Operation Horseshoe) to drive the Kosovar Albanian population out of Kosovo.

What we also know is that he tried to implement this brutal strategy of ethnic cleansing, but failed. Those refugees are now home. Instead of hiding in hills, sitting in refugee camps, or being scattered throughout Europe, the vast majority of Kosovar Albanians were brought home within months. In comparison, in Bosnia and Herzegovina, there are still an estimated one-third of a million refugees, with over twice that number internally displaced. The firm and timely response of NATO and the international community stopped a vicious spiral of violence in its tracks.

## Note

1. Bosnia and Herzegovina went to war with Serbia in the 1990s.

# Canada Should Not Have Participated in the Unjust NATO Air Campaign

## Sinclair Stevens

*Sinclair Stevens is a Canadian lawyer, businessman, and former member of Parliament. In the following viewpoint, he argues that the bombing of Serbia by NATO was an act of aggression. He says the NATO bombing killed civilians and increased genocidal action on the ground. Canada's participation in NATO's act of aggressive warfare goes against Canadian traditions and morals, Stevens argues. The real reason for the war was not humanitarian, he claims. Instead, he says, NATO was eager to find a new mission after the end of the Cold War, and arms manufacturers encouraged the attack because they were afraid of a military drawdown.*

History will remember 1999 as the year when Canada shifted from being a world-renowned peacekeeper to an aggressor nation. How will they judge us, knowing that Canada undertook this tremendous paradigm shift without parliamentary consent and certainly without the approval of the Canadian people?

# Innocent Casualties and Genocide

The new role was dramatized on July 1 [1999] during the Canada Day Celebrations, when Prime Minister Jean Chretien, before the Peace Tower on Parliament Hill, called on Canadians to honour our brave heroes who had joined in the NATO [North Atlantic Treaty Organization] bombing of Yugoslavia.

Later, some of those airmen expressed the sentiment that they were not, in fact, heroes, but that they had simply carried out their orders. Theirs was the more accurate account.

Do you call NATO airmen heroes, when their bombing raids resulted in these tragedies?

- April 14, 64 Albanian refugees were killed in the NATO bombing of Kosovo road convoys;

- April 23, another 10 were killed when NATO missiles hit a Serbian state television station in Belgrade;

- May 7, three were killed in NATO's bombing of the Chinese embassy in Belgrade;

- May 13, more than 80 Albanian civilians were killed in the NATO bombing of the Kosovo village of Korisa;

- May 30, nine were killed when NATO bombed a bridge in Varvarin, central Serbia.

Is it appropriate to commend NATO actions that resulted in serious environmental disasters when fuel refineries, storage tanks and chemical factories were blown up, or to commend NATO when more genocide was carried out and more refugees fled Kosovo after NATO's actions began, than had occurred before NATO intervened?

NATO's spin artists call the campaign a victory. A victory over what? It is a strange victory when we remember that the two demands in the schedule to the Rambouillet agreement [a peace deal Serbs rejected] that helped trigger the war, have now been abandoned by NATO.

## Searching for a Mission

In any event, it was no contest. The NATO alliance, with more than 70 per cent of the world's military strike force and a combined gross national product a thousand times the size of Serbia, could not lose. In relative economic terms, it is like crushing Nova Scotia. For NATO to use such might, and cause such devastation in the name of peace, reminds us of Calgacus, the Caledonian leader, who in 84 A.D. rallied his troops against Roman invaders by declaring "They create a wasteland and call it peace." While Rome won the ensuing battle of the Grampians, they never did conquer Scotland, but instead Emperor Hadrian subsequently built his stone wall.

Kosovo was used as a conventional justification for action by the NATO alliance to give them a new mission now that there is no longer a cold war. Since the cold war ended, the sales of arms manufacturers has fallen in real terms by 25 per cent.

At a conference celebrating NATO's 50th anniversary, held last February [1999] in Toronto at the Canadian Forces College, several speakers stressed that without a new mission NATO would be out of business.

Kosovo was subsequently welcomed as a rallying point to help NATO re-shape its mandate.

Politicians, the press, and the public have all been orchestrated to accept this new aggressive role.

It is a dangerous precedent.

It is particularly dangerous when we realize it is inspired by the armament manufacturers who have witnessed slumping sales since the cold war ended. They are one of the most powerful lobbies in the democratic world and it is they who have triumphed in identifying a new NATO role. Their cash registers are ringing again.

## The Power of Arms Manufacturers

Just how powerful are these armament companies and consortiums? Take Lockheed Martin Corporation for example. If you are

## The Bombing of the Chinese Embassy in Belgrade

The Chinese Embassy in Belgrade was accidentally bombed by NATO forces on 7 May 1999. Prior to this incident the US had been working hard to maintain positive relations with a rising China. Chinese crackdowns against internal dissidents and the US plans for a regional missile shield to deflect missile attacks in East Asia all had been hot points for the bilateral relationship in the run up to Kosovo. The NATO operation and the subsequent accidental bombing of the Chinese Embassy in Belgrade caused the situation to deteriorate. There were attempts to patch up the bilateral relationship following the intervention, but the evidence of long-term damage was clear. The *Foreign Affairs Journal*, published by the Chinese People's Institute of Foreign Affairs, a mouthpiece for the government, included a number of markedly anti-US articles such as "NATO Lifts Its Mask of Humanitarianism" and "NATO's New Strategic Concept Threatens World Peace." Beijing was clearly not pleased with the NATO operation in Kosovo, even if it was half a world away.

*Michael J. Williams, NATO, Security and Risk Management: From Kosovo to Khandahar. New York: Routledge, 2009, p. 59.*

shopping for a jet fighter, check them out. Lockheed's high-profile weapons systems include jet fighters such as the F16, the F22 and the joint strike fighter. Other high-tech offerings include missiles.

Lockheed is conveniently based in Maryland, just outside Washington, D.C., and it employs 165,000 employees, which helps in lobbying. In 1998, it sold $18 billion of product to the U.S. government and $5 billion to other governments. In total, 89 per cent of their sales were to governments. In the same year, Serbia's GDP [gross domestic product] was $15 billion (all figures in U.S. dollars).

Raytheon Company is another happy supplier of weapons. Their name stands for "light of the Gods." A fistful of Tomahawk missiles in one hand and Patriots in the other, Raytheon hurls tonnes of firepower into the arsenals of the U.S. military. Raytheon has a U.S. government contract to produce smart bombs that can be dropped up to 40 nautical miles from targets. It employs 108,000 people and is situated in Massachusetts, with sales of more than $20 billion.

Then there is the Northrop Grumman Corporation in California, which builds the F14 Tomcat fighter. Seventy five per cent of its sales ($7 billion) are to the U.S. government.

Lockheed and Northrop Grumman are so pleased with their relationship with NATO they bought three full-page advertisements in a survey of NATO entitled "Knights in shining armour," published in the *Economist* on April 24. Lockheed's double spread advertisement screamed out "For a strong alliance—build more bridges." It didn't mention that its weapons helped blow up bridges in Serbia. Northrop Grumman's one-page highlighted its stealth technology.

Great Britain has British Aerospace, which is Europe's largest defence contractor and No. 3 in the world. It employs 48,000 people with sales to 72 countries, including 23 friendly air forces. France has Thompson CSF which operated with a military bearing, employing 46,000 people with 64 per cent of its sales in aerospace and other defence electronic products.

There is a European consortium producing the Eurofighter Typhoon, which also bought a full-page ad in the *Economist* survey. The consortium sees a global market of some 800 combat aircraft over the period 2005 to 2025, worth more than $70 billion, and it hopes to capture 50 per cent of that market.

## The Danger of NATO

When the Berlin Wall came down, it was evident the cold war was over.[1] Now NATO, with its new unilateral aggressive stance, is creating new hot points. This is the most dangerous world development since the end of the cold war. NATO is undermining the United Nations. It has already created friction with Russia, antagonized China, and encouraged other minor despots to seek nuclear weapons, as a deterrent should NATO target them.

Canada's reason for joining in this aggression is difficult to understand. We are not a significant armament manufacturer such as the United States, Great Britain, or France. So we are not pressured by the arms lobby, and employment is not an issue.

Since 1947, we have participated in nearly 50 United Nations–led peacekeeping missions, yet now we have joined in an undeclared war against a sovereign nation. We engaged in the Gulf War [against Iraq in the early 1990s] and in the Korean War [against North Korea in the 1950s] to resist aggression. Now we have become an aggressor.

The arguments used to justify bombing Serbia could be used to support similar aggression in many other countries, where there is horrible genocide and millions of refugees who live without hope.

No one questions that greater efforts should be made to solve these problems.

Perhaps a new United Nations mandated commission could be constituted that would bring financial assistance to any government that agrees to co-operate and clean up these tragic situations.

Rather than spend more than $20 billion in devastating Serbia, which has lowered its GDP by 40 per cent, a $2 billion a year Marshall Plan–type aid program for six years would at least double its GDP.

## No Aggression in the Name of Peace

Defensive military alliances such as NATO should not be allowed to become aggressors in the name of peace. That was not NATO's mandate when it was founded 50 years ago, after significant urging by Canada's Lester Pearson, and Louis St. Laurent.

If NATO is allowed to follow this path, it will lead us to a major world conflict, in which only the arms makers will win.

Speaking of "knights in shining armour," the present millennium began with the crusades that justified human slaughter in the [name] of "just causes."

It would be a great tragedy if history were to repeat itself at the dawn of the next millennium.

## Note

1. The Cold War was the conflict between the West and Communist Russia that ended in the late 1980s. The Berlin Wall was a barrier that separated democratic West Berlin from Communist East Berlin. It was torn down in 1989.

# The Milosevic Trial Was a Success for International Justice

*Aryeh Neier*

*Aryeh Neier is a human rights activist and the president of the Open Society Foundations. In the following viewpoint, Neier argues that international criminal proceedings such as those against former Serbian president Slobodan Milosevic are very difficult and costly. Nonetheless, he says, even though Milosevic died before his trial was completed, the trial process was still important. Neier points to other prosecutions that resulted in convictions and says that worldwide officials who commit genocide or other crimes now know that they may face justice. Neier also argues that the trial against Milosevic revealed important evidence of crimes. Such revelations, he says, could help convict others guilty of war crimes.*

Slobodan Milosevic cheated justice, and by doing so demonstrated the futility of attempting to deal with war crimes and crimes against humanity through international prosecutions.

Aryeh Neier, "Milosevic Trial Not in Vain," Open Society Foundations, March 24, 2006. www.soros.org. Copyright © 2006 by Project Syndicate. All rights reserved. Reproduced by permission.

*Former Serbian president Slobodan Milosevic refuses the presence of a lawyer during his initial hearing before the International Criminal Tribunal for the Former Yugoslavia in 2001. While some believe the ICTY was unsuccessful, others argue that it served as a model for future international courts.* © Raphael Gaillarde/Gamma-Rapho via Getty Images.

That, at least, is the conclusion that some people have reached after Milosevic's death in a Hague prison: the fact that he was able to drag out his trial for four years and still escape a verdict is considered proof that the international community is wasting its resources by putting such people on trial for their misdeeds.

Even the most dedicated partisans of international justice concede that the International Criminal Tribunal for the Former Yugoslavia (ICTY) has had many shortcomings. All those associated with it were new to such proceedings, and had to learn on the job, as there had been no such bodies since the courts at Nuremberg and Tokyo after World War II.

Moreover, the post-WWII bodies were tribunals in which the war's victors judged the losers, and those prosecuted were already in custody. The ICTY, by contrast, has no capacity of its own to arrest defendants.

It must rely on persuasion to secure cooperation by others—cooperation that is still being withheld in the case of the two most notorious defendants from the Bosnian War, Radovan Karadzic and Ratko Mladic.

Until Tony Blair and Robin Cook became, respectively, Prime Minister and Foreign Secretary of the United Kingdom in 1997, four years after the ICTY was established, NATO troops in Bosnia failed to arrest indicted suspects even when they ran into them.

By now, of course, 133 defendants from all parties to the wars in ex-Yugoslavia have appeared before the Tribunal, charged with war crimes, crimes against humanity, and even genocide.

These are highly complex cases, frequently involving not only novel issues under international law, but also thousands of witnesses—often traumatised by their suffering—dispersed to many lands, the constant need for high-quality simultaneous translations, and disruptive tactics by some defendants.

Yet the proceedings against 85 of them, including appeals, have been completed.

In trying them, the ICTY has been a model of fairness at all times.

The mountains of evidence in its records make the horrendous crimes committed in the wars in ex-Yugoslavia comparable in the extent of their documentation to those by the Nazis.

Inevitable efforts by demagogues to revise the history of what took place in ex-Yugoslavia in the 1990s will be complicated by the availability of that evidence, including the facts compiled during the Milosevic trial.

Far from being a failure, the ICTY has inspired the establishment of several other such courts, including those for Rwanda, Sierra Leone, Cambodia, and the permanent International Criminal Court.

Even heads of state have not escaped these bodies.

Milosevic, the former president of Yugoslavia, and then Serbia, died in prison.

Biljana Plavsic, the President of the Bosnian Serb Republic after Karadzic, expressed remorse for her crimes, pleaded guilty, and is serving a prison sentence.

Jean Kambanda, former Prime Minister of Rwanda, pleaded guilty to crimes against humanity and genocide and is serving a life sentence in prison.

We are thus slowly reaching the point where some of those contemplating crimes such as those committed by Slobodan Milosevic must recognise that one day they could be held accountable.

Charles Taylor was President of Liberia when the Tribunal for Sierra Leone indicted him.

He had to flee his country, paving the way for the democratic transition that resulted in the recent election of Ellen Johnson Sirleaf. Taylor still faces the prospect of trial and, another former dictator, Saddam Hussein, is now on trial before a national court in Iraq.

Persisting on the path of international justice will continue to require substantial resources.

Great as they are, the costs are trivial in comparison to the expense of humanitarian aid, international military intervention, and reconstruction assistance.

Most important, of course, is the need to prevent the suffering caused by the crimes that lead to international prosecutions; and when those crimes cannot be prevented, we must provide some comfort and redress to the victims and their families by doing justice.

Of course, the slow, tortuous process of international justice is often frustrating to the victims.

But it would be worse if those responsible for great crimes got away with it, as happened all too often in the past.

In the wake of Milosevic's death, Karadzic and Mladic should be brought before the ICTY, both to reinforce its work and to demonstrate to their victims that the international community is resolved not to allow their suffering to be forgotten.

The ICTY's mission is as valid and as vital as ever: to show that the era of impunity for some of humanity's worst crimes is coming to an end.

# The Milosevic Trial Turned into an Embarrassing Spectacle

*Michael P. Scharf*

*Michael P. Scharf is the director of the international law center at Case Western Reserve University School of Law. In the following viewpoint, he argues that the trial of former Serbian president Slobodan Milosevic was undignified and embarrassing. The main problem, he says, was that Milosevic was allowed to represent himself in court. As a result, the trial was slowed down by Milosevic's poor health. In addition, he says, Milosevic used the platform given him by self-representation to harangue the court, browbeat witnesses, and make his case to the Serbian public. Milosevic, Scharf argues, was able to sway public opinion in Serbia in his favor. This was especially harmful, Scharf says, because the trial was meant to lead the Serbian public to acknowledge its government's complicity in war crimes. Scharf concludes that counsel should have been appointed for Milosevic.*

Almost everyone knows the old legal saying: "He who represents himself has a fool for a client and an idiot for a lawyer." The trial of former Serbian leader Slobodan Milosevic suggests a

Michael P. Scharf, "Making a Spectacle of Himself," *Washington Post*, August 29, 2004.

related adage: "A judge who permits a rogue leader to represent himself in an international war crimes trial is just as misguided."

## An Erroneous Ruling

On Tuesday [August 31, 2004], Milosevic's trial—more than two years old and counting—is scheduled to resume before the International Criminal Tribunal in The Hague [Netherlands]. The opening act of the trial's new phase will be the judges' announcement of their decision on whether to allow Milosevic to continue acting as his own lawyer.

At the start of the trial in February 2002, the original presiding judge, Britain's Richard May, ruled that "under international law, the defendant has a right to counsel, but he also has a right not to have counsel." Virtually everything that has gone wrong with the Milosevic trial can be traced back to that erroneous ruling.

The decision has caused the trial to drag on twice as long as anticipated. Because of concerns about Milosevic's high blood pressure (240 over 120), the judges have had to scale back the length and frequency of the proceedings to ensure that the former leader is not "tried to death." As a result, the trial takes place only three times a week as opposed to the standard five; the number of hours per day has been reduced from eight to four; and there are frequent lengthy recesses to allow the defendant-lawyer to regain his strength. These delays have taken their toll on justice. Judge May recently died of cancer and a replacement had to be found; witness memories are fading; and the international community is losing interest.

## The Court of Public Opinion

The judges have given Milosevic wider latitude than an ordinary defendant or lawyer. Normally, the accused addresses the court only when he takes the stand to give testimony, and he must take an oath to tell the truth. Moreover, he is limited to offering evidence that is relevant to the charges, and is subject to cross-examination by the prosecution. By acting as his own counsel,

## The Early Years and Political Rise of Slobodan Milosevic

Slobodan Milosevic was born on August 20, 1941, in Pozarevac, Yugoslavia. His father, a Communist and teacher who studied to become a Serbian Orthodox priest, abandoned his family early and later killed himself. His mother, also an ardent Communist and teacher, took her life in 1974. An uncle also committed suicide. Milosevic met his future wife Mirjana Markovic—whose family was high ranking in the Serbian Communist community—while in high school. They married shortly afterward and raised two children. Milosevic and Mirjana were often described as "political partners"; indeed, many in political circles believe Mirjana—a professor of Marxist sociology at the University of Belgrade—was "the power behind the throne."

Milosevic's rise to the top of the Communist hierarchy in Yugoslavia was unremarkable at first. While at the University of Belgrade he was active in the university chapter of the League of Communists. His mentor was Ivan Stambolic, a nephew of one of the most powerful Serbian Communist leaders and Milosevic's uncle

Milosevic was able to begin the trial with an 18-hour-long opening argument, which included Hollywood-quality video and slide-show presentations showing the destruction wrought by the 1999 NATO bombing campaign.

As his own defense counsel, Milosevic has been able to treat the witnesses, prosecutors and judges in a manner that would earn ordinary defense counsel a citation or incarceration for contempt of court. In addition to regularly making disparaging remarks about the court and browbeating witnesses, Milosevic pontificates at length during cross-examination of every witness, despite repeated warnings from the bench. Milosevic, who by marriage. Stambolic, five years older than Milosevic, once headed Technogas, a state gas company. In 1973, when Stambolic moved on to Beobanka, the capital's biggest bank, Milosevic took over Technogas. When Stambolic left the bank to become prime minister of Serbia, Milosevic succeeded him there, too. In 1982 Milosevic became a member of the collective presidency of the League of Communists of Serbia and two years later the head of the Belgrade Communist Party. The collective presidency of the League of Communists of Serbia elected Milosevic as its president in 1986.

On April 24, 1987, in the independent Yugoslavian province of Kosovo, Slobodan Milosevic witnessed local Albanian police beating Serb protesters. They were among calm crowds who were protesting the continuing mistreatment of Serbs by the Albanian majority. Milosevic stepped out onto a balcony and shouted, "No one will dare to beat you again!" Almost immediately the tide of Serbian politics shifted and, according to Milosevic biographer Slavoljub Djukic in *Time*, "In less than a year [Milosevic] moved from being a second-rate politician to almost a god."

Just months after the 1987 balcony appearance in Kosovo, Milosevic succeeded in removing Stambolic from the national party presidency, and Stambolic loyalists from party positions. Stambolic disappeared from public life. In 1989 Milosevic became president of Serbia.

spends his nights at the tribunal's detention center, has no incentive to heed the judges' admonitions.

Milosevic's caustic defense strategy is unlikely to win him an acquittal, but it isn't aimed at the court of law in The Hague. His audience is the court of public opinion back home in Serbia, where the trial is a top-rated TV show and Milosevic's standing continues to rise.

Opinion polls have reported that 75 percent of Serbs do not feel that Milosevic is getting a fair trial, and 67 percent think that he is not responsible for any war crimes. "Sloba Hero!" graffiti is omnipresent on Belgrade buses and buildings. Last

*An ethnic Albanian family in Kosovo watches the trial of former Serbian president Slobodan Milosevic on television in 2002. Milosevic's popularity increased in Serbia, where the trial was a top-rated TV show. © AP Images/Visar Kryeziu.*

December, he easily won a seat in the Serbian parliament in a national election.

In creating the Yugoslavia tribunal statute, the U.N. Security Council set three objectives: first, to educate the Serbian people, who were long misled by Milosevic's propaganda, about the acts of aggression, war crimes and crimes against humanity committed by his regime; second, to facilitate national reconciliation by pinning prime responsibility on Milosevic and other top leaders and disclosing the ways in which the Milosevic regime had induced ordinary Serbs to commit atrocities; and third, to promote political catharsis while enabling Serbia's newly elected leaders to distance themselves from the repressive policies of the past. May's decision to allow Milosevic to represent himself has seriously undercut these aims.

## The Dignity of the Courtroom

May felt he had no choice in the matter because the tribunal's legal charter stated that the defendant has the right "to defend himself in person or through legal assistance of his own choosing." But some experts—and I'm including myself—are now arguing that May got the law wrong.

The language from the Yugoslavia tribunal statute originally comes from a human rights treaty known as the International Covenant on Civil and Political Rights. The negotiating record of the International Covenant indicates that the drafters' concern was with *effective* representation, not self-representation. In other words, the drafters felt that a defendant should have a right to either be represented by a lawyer or to represent himself; they did not state that each defendant must be asked to choose between the two. Unlike Britain and the United States, most countries of the world do not allow criminal defendants to represent themselves under any circumstances, and this has been deemed consistent with international law by the European Court of Human Rights.

Even if May was correct in his reading of the law as providing a right to self-representation, he was wrong to treat that right as absolute. As authority for his position, May cited the U.S. Supreme Court's 1975 ruling in *Feratta v. California*, which held that there was a fundamental right to self-representation in U.S. courts. But the high court also added a caveat, which May overlooked, stating that "a right of self-representation is not a license to abuse the dignity of the courtroom." U.S. appellate courts have subsequently held that the right of self-representation is subject to exceptions—such as when the defendant acts in a disruptive manner, when self-representation interferes with the dignity of the proceedings or when the issues in the case are too complex for a defendant to represent himself adequately.

Milosevic's antics and poor health have repeatedly disrupted the trial, justifying appointment of counsel to represent him in court for the remainder of the proceedings. There's precedent for taking such a step: In the trial of former Serbian paramilitary leader Vojislav Seselj, the Yugoslavia tribunal required Seselj—over his objection—to accept "stand-by counsel," ready to step in as soon as the defendant became disruptive or the issues became too complex.

## Appoint Counsel

In a sense, the tribunal has already appointed standby counsel for Milosevic in the guise of Stephen Kay and the other amicus ("friends of the court") counsel. While not bound to follow the defendant's directives, their job has been to ensure that legal arguments favoring the defense are presented to the judges. It would be a small step to transform the amicus counsel into a full-blown defense team, and instruct it to represent Milosevic for the rest of the trial. The lawyers are already intimately familiar with the case and are willing to take on such a role. And unlike Milosevic, they will be bound to play by the rules.

If, on the other hand, the tribunal rules that Milosevic still has a right to represent himself, the precedent will affect other international cases. Saddam Hussein, whose war crimes trial is set to begin later this year, will be able to argue that he, too, has a right to represent himself before the Iraqi Special Tribunal.

If Hussein were allowed to follow Milosevic's playbook—using the unique opportunity of self-representation to launch daily attacks against the legitimacy of the proceedings and the U.S. invasion of Iraq—this would seriously undermined the goal of fostering reconciliation between the Iraqi Kurds, Shiites and Sunnis.[1] The historic record developed by such a trial would forever be questioned. And the trial would transform Hussein and his subordinates into martyrs, potentially fueling violent opposition to the new Iraqi government.

Justice demands that Milosevic and Hussein be given fair trials. That can best be guaranteed by appointing distinguished counsel to defend them, not by permitting them to act as their own lawyers.

## Note

1. The Kurds are an ethnic minority in Iraq; Sunni and Shi'a are denominations of Islam.

# Europe Should Recognize an Independent Kosovo

## *The Economist*

*The* Economist *is a British news publication. In the following viewpoint, the* Economist *argues that it is logical for Europe to support independence for Kosovo but not for other breakaway groups in Transdniestria, South Ossetia, and Abkhazia. The* Economist *argues that Kosovo wants to join the European Union (EU) and is looking for Europe to shape its future institutions. Areas like Transdniestria, on the other hand, are looking to Russia for support and guidance. As a result, the* Economist *says, Kosovo has a better chance of becoming democratic and prosperous like Europe. This is a goal Europe supports because the EU believes that a more European Kosovo would be a better neighbor than a more Russian South Ossetia or Abkhazia.*

Why is the West giving Kosovo independence when it refuses to recognise Transdniestria, South Ossetia and Abkhazia? These three places are nominally independent—at least in their own eyes—and have been so for many years.

## Kosovo and the European Union

At first sight it seems a clear case of Western double standards. Kosovar Albanians don't want to be under Serbian rule any more than the Abkhaz feel Georgian or the Transdniestrians like Moldova. They have established their status by force of arms, and entrenched it over ten years of quasi-independence. Is not the real story just an American power-play in Europe, punishing Serbia and rewarding the only pro-American Muslims in the world?

Nobody would deny that such political calculations have influenced decision-making. But the real difference is another one. Kosovo wants to join the European Union [EU]. That much is at least clear, however badly run Kosovo may be at the moment, and however much gangsterism and ethno-nationalism have flourished there under the haphazard stewardship of the so-called international community. Kosovo does not want to join, say, Turkey in a new "Ottoman Caliphate". Nor is it even interested in forming a "Greater Albania".

That makes a big difference. Transdniestria, Abkhazia and South Ossetia do not subscribe to the Euroatlantic vision of multilateral security and law-governed political freedom. The main priority of the ruling elites there is self-enrichment, followed by at least a rhetorical commitment to closer integration with Russia (a goal that the Kremlin endorses in theory but seems remarkably cautious about in practice).

The West is reluctant to say so bluntly, but that makes a difference. The EU is sending thousands of lawyers, prosecutors and police officers to Kosovo, in what might be termed the continent's most ambitious colonial adventure for decades. That "soft imperialism" creates at least a chance of success for Kosovo's independence.

All this may yet be derailed. Bosnia [a former Yugoslav republic] is falling apart again; Macedonia [another former Yugoslav republic] still looks fragile; and Russia could not ask for more fertile soil for mischief, with Europe divided and indecisive. But it is worth a try.

"Little Birdy," cartoon by Christo Komarnitski, February 16, 2008. www.CagleCartoons .com. Copyright © by Christo Komarnitski, Bulgaria, and CagleCartoons.com. All rights reserved.

## Russia Has Less to Offer

Contrast that with Transdniestria or Abkhazia. Imagine that Russia and a bunch of other countries—Belarus, Uzbekistan, Armenia and Venezuela, say—decided to go ahead and recognise these breakaway statelets. It is almost laughable to imagine what such outside supporters could offer to promote the rule of law and good government. Would Hugo Chávez of Venezuela offer policemen? Would Russia provide prosecutors, or Uzbekistan start teaching Abkhaz civil servants about e-government?

This is the weakness at the heart of all the Kremlin's foreign-policy efforts in the countries of the former Soviet Union. It offers a great deal for elites. Some enjoy lavish hospitality and lucrative directorships. Others get intelligence co-operation and sales of advanced weaponry.

But Russia has much less to offer from the public's point of view. True, it offers passports, and a Russian passport is not worthless.

But the survival of the Soviet-era *propiska* system [restricting residence rights in Russia] means that this does not confer the prized right to live and work in Moscow. Even the Kremlin's most loyal allies can't offer that to their citizens as a quid pro quo. (Admittedly, Schengen[1] and American visas can still be shamefully hard to come by, even for citizens of ex-captive nations that are loyally Euroatlantic in outlook).

What the EU will not say, but thinks privately, is this: We are supporting Kosovo's independence because of the chance that it will become more like us, and hence a better neighbour. We oppose independence for Transdniestria et al because it would make them more like Russia, and therefore worse for Europe.

## Note

1. The Schengen Agreement, covering twenty-five European countries, eliminates all internal border controls, enabling travelers to cross those borders without showing a passport.

# It Would Be a Mistake to Recognize an Independent Kosovo

*Thomas Landen*

*Thomas Landen is a writer for the* Brussels Journal. *In the following viewpoint, he argues that the Kosovar Albanians fighting for independence have historic ties to radical Islamic groups and the international terrorist group al Qaeda. In addition, he says, the Kosovo Liberation Army (KLA), which fought for independence in Kosovo, is linked to drug running, slave trafficking, and criminal gangs. Landen argues that an independent Kosovo would be a haven for radical Islam and mob activities. He says the United States and European nations that support Kosovo independence are setting themselves up for disaster. Landen worries that the result might even lead to a European war, pitting Russia, China, and other opponents of Kosovo's independence against the United States, many European Union nations, and Osama bin Laden. In such a war, he says, Western European nations like Britain, France, and Germany are positioning themselves on the wrong side.*

Today [February 18, 2008], one day after Kosovo's unilateral declaration of independence, the United States and the major

*Waving Serbian flags, Kosovo Serbs protest Kosovo's declaration of independence in February 2008.* © Carsten Koall/Getty Images News/Getty Images.

European countries rushed to recognize Kosovo's independence. [US president] George Bush hailed Kosovo's "bold and historic bid for statehood." Five years ago, Mr Bush invaded Iraq and began "operation Iraqi freedom." He toppled Saddam Hussein in order to get rid of a rogue regime, one of the members of the "axis of evil."[1] Five years later, Mr Bush is saddling Europe with a new rogue state.

## The KLA and al-Qa'eda

Surely, Mr Bush knows that al-Qa'eda fighters were involved in driving the Serbs from Kosovo in the late 1990s. The *Jerusalem Post* reported in 1998 that the Kosovo Liberation Army (KLA) was "provided with financial and military support from Islamic countries," and had been "bolstered by hundreds of Iranian fighters or mujahedin [some of whom] were trained in [al-Qaeda leader] Osama bin Laden's terrorist camps in Afghanistan." There is more proof of involvement of the KLA of the (then and current) Kosovar leader Hashim Thaçi, nicknamed 'the Snake,' with al-Qaeda than there was of the Iraqi Ba'ath regime of the late Saddam Hussein.

Yesterday, thousands of ethnic Albanians were celebrating their independence in the Kosovar capital Pristina, shouting "KLA! KLA!" and waving American flags alongside the Albanian and the new Kosovar national flag. Is America now in league with al-Qaeda and the Albanian mafia? What is the point of fighting Islamism in Iraq while at the same time one creates a free haven for Islamists on the European continent?

Surely, Mr Bush knows that [as stated by Slobodan Milosevic] "the KLA . . . is tied in with every known middle and far eastern drug cartel. Interpol, Europol, and nearly every European intelligence and counter-narcotics agency has files open on drug syndicates that lead right to the KLA, and right to Albanian gangs in [Kosovo]. Furthermore, the KLA was involved in sex slaves. Furthermore, they were supported by Osama Bin Laden."

Only last week, General Fabio Mini, the Italian general who commanded the NATO troops in Kosovo in 2002–2003, warned that the recognition of Kosovo's independence would turn out to be a "fatal mistake." This new state, the general said, will only benefit the clans who currently rule Kosovo: i.e. the clans of the current Prime Minister, Hashim 'the Snake' Thaçi "who is in business with the oil companies," of his predecessor Ramush Haradinay, who is standing trial for war crimes in The Hague, of former Prime Minister Agim Ceku "who wants to become a generalissimo" and of Behgjet Pacolli, a billionaire "who needs somewhere to stack the money of his empire." "What these clans want," General Mini said, "is a place in Europe where they can open new banks, a free haven for the money that flows in from the East."

## A Fatal Mistake

Sadly, Mr Bush is not the only one making a "fatal mistake." Many of the 27 European Union (EU) member states have done so, too, including the big three—Britain, France, Germany—and the Franco-German poodle, multinational Belgium. Others, however, have serious misgivings. Spain, Cyprus, Greece, Bulgaria, Romania and Slovakia oppose Kosovo's independence. The Italian government is divided on the issue.

In a statement issued in Brussels the EU foreign ministers say that Kosovo's history of "conflict, ethnic cleansing and humanitarian catastrophe" in the 1990s by Serbia exempts it from the rule that international borders can only be changed with the agreement of all parties. The EU countries that recognize Kosovo's independence admit that they are doing so in violation of the rule of "territorial integrity" of nations under international law. They want to 'punish' Serbia for its misbehaviour in the 1990s, but fail to see that they are 'punishing' the whole of Europe by saddling it with a state run by criminal gangs.

Russia refuses to accept Kosovo's independence. So does China. Moscow has called on the United Nations to annul [Kosovo capital] Pristina's decision. It will be interesting to see which countries will back Russia in the UN. Moscow's allies in the Organization of Islamic States definitely will not. They applaud the establishment of a new Muslim state in Europe. Will Russia now become the leader of the Europeans who resist the Islamization of their continent? Or will the crisis in the Balkans trigger a new world war, just as the Great War [World War I] was triggered in the Balkans in 1914?

Indeed, what will Russia do if the 16,000 NATO "peace keeping" troops in Kosovo attack the Serbian army when it attempts to recover its breakaway province? If Russia intervenes, then 2008 might become the year that war broke out between Russia and NATO. America, the EU, Europe's immigrant "youths" and Osama bin Laden would find themselves on one side, and Russia, with China and the Europeans who resist Islamization on the other.

## Note

1. Bush referred to Iraq, Iran, and North Korea as an "axis of evil."

CHAPTER 3

# Personal Narratives

# Chapter Exercises

## 1. Writing Prompt

Imagine you are an ethnic Albanian who witnessed Serb violence. Write a one-page diary entry explaining what you saw and describing your thoughts.

## 2. Group Activity

Form groups and develop five interview questions that could be asked of Serbs who lived through the NATO bombings during the Kosovo conflict.

# A Peace Worker Is Jailed in Prewar Kosovo

*Peter Lippman*

*Peter Lippman is a US human rights activist. In the following viewpoint, he discusses his experiences in Kosovo in 1998 before the Kosovo War. He talks about the severe repression inflicted on Albanians by Serbs. For instance, he says, Albanians were forced out of most professions and were subject to interrogation and beatings on the street. He describes massive peaceful protests by Albanians and notes the rise of a militant resistance movement, the Kosovo Liberation Army. He also discusses his imprisonment and the terrible conditions for Albanians in Serb prisons. He concludes by arguing for more Western pressure to end Serbian abuses, and he asserts that Slobodan Milosevic, the Serb leader, should be tried for war crimes.*

I traveled to Pristina, capital of the southern Yugoslav province of Kosovo, last month as an affiliate of the California-based organization Peaceworkers. We met with Kosovo Albanians and Serbs, and observed massive demonstrations by Albanians who were protesting the recent massacre in the nearby Drenica region.

Our visit culminated in our unexpected arrest. We were detained and summarily sentenced to 10 days in jail for failure to register our presence in Pristina with the local police. An American diplomat trying to get us released likened this infraction to "tearing the tag off a mattress."

Peaceworkers came to Kosovo as observers on the invitation of the Independent Student Union, one of the leaders of the current series of protests. While in Pristina, we met with a variety of people who are active in holding together the largely underground infrastructure of Albanian society: professors, doctors, journalists and human-rights workers.

Kosovo's population is 90 percent Albanian. As Peaceworkers met with professors, doctors, journalists, human-rights workers and ordinary citizens, we learned how in the late 1980s, Serbian President Slobodan Milosevic removed Kosovo's constitutional status as an autonomous province. In the following years, Albanian teachers and professors were removed from the schools, doctors and nurses from the hospitals, and most workers were fired from their jobs. The result was the destruction of Kosovo's economy.

The dean of the philology faculty of Pristina's underground university explained to us how, in 1991, the Serbian regime had imposed an exclusively Serbian-language curriculum. When the Albanian professors refused to teach this curriculum, they were fired. High-school teachers and university professors soon set up a parallel educational system in private rooms, basements and storefronts. We visited an advanced English class in an unheated, empty store. Boxes of bottles lined the back of the room. The students sat on makeshift wooden benches, wearing their coats, hats and gloves. The young teacher shivered as she gave a lesson in prefixes: neo-liberalism, neo-colonialism. Pan-Hellenic, pan-Balkan.

During a visit to Mother Teresa Clinic, the only free OB-Gyn facility in Kosovo, we heard how in 1990, police had entered the hospital in Pristina and fired doctors and nurses with no notice,

*Peter Lippman (second from the right) stands with other American activists after their release from a Kosovo prison in 1998. Lippman's imprisonment allowed him to see firsthand the atrocities inflicted on Albanians in Serb prisons.* © AP Images/Boris Grdanoski.

even in the middle of operations, beating those who protested. The clinic we visited represents a valiant effort at creating a parallel medical system but is pitifully inadequate for a population of 2 million. Women who have given birth share beds for lack of space and must leave the clinic two hours later. We saw three newborns heated by plastic soft-drink bottles filled with warm water. Most women give birth at home now, and the infant mortality rate has more than doubled.

In the nine years since the Serbian government removed Kosovo's autonomous status, repression has constantly increased. For most of that period, Albanians have feared to protest their loss of rights, due to the possibility of violent reprisal. Indeed, random violence against Albanians is the rule. The young dental student with whose family I stayed was recently taken off the bus by a policeman and beaten on the street for possessing a library card, evidence of his attendance in the parallel university system. A high-school pupil I met had been beaten for not being able to speak the Serbian language. And last month's massacre at

Drenica, where the police killed around 100 men, women and children, was only the most recent of many atrocities against villagers.

The Albanians' response to the Serbian government's destruction of their social infrastructure and repression has been passive until recently. But presently, two options have appeared: the Kosovo Liberation Army and the nonviolent protest movement led by the students. From inside Kosovo, it appears that the army, most likely a few armed groups in the villages, has no chance of posing a serious threat to the regime, and a strong likelihood of suffering more massacres. Villages in the Drenica area and further west continue to be attacked today by an army masquerading as a police force.

At the same time, my colleagues and I daily witnessed peaceful rallies numbering up to 200,000. Accompanied by journalists and other foreign observers, these demonstrations have managed to encourage defiance of the police state and send a message of resistance that the world has had little opportunity to hear until now. The images of thousands of demonstrators sitting down in the street in front of a line of heavily armed policemen, and of 20,000 women trying to march to Drenica with bread for the villagers in their hands, will stay with me forever. We would do well to support and encourage this grass-roots movement before more Albanians lose their patience and turn to a more dangerous path.

The day I left Pristina to return to Sarajevo, I was taken off the bus and arrested. The police placed me in a room with seven Albanian men who had also been arrested that day. What I saw when I walked into that cell shocked me. The seven men, required to stand in line with their heads down and their hands behind their backs whenever a guard entered, had the most demoralized air I had ever encountered among human beings. It was clear that some of them had been beaten; I could tell by their swollen hands and the bruises I later witnessed in the shower. There wasn't much point in asking the reason; there is none. In the evening of my first day, guards came in regularly, and I saw them slap a boy who could not have been older than 16, for not speaking the Serbian language. Another young man was struck for having attended one of the demonstrations.

Upon strong pressure from our embassy, we Americans were freed after a few days. But life goes on in Kosovo; for the Albanians the difference between being in and out of jail is not as great as one would wish. Kosovo needs more attention from humanitarian-aid organizations, international journalists and human-rights observers. And the West must bear down on the Serbian regime to negotiate with the Kosovo Albanians without preconditions and with an international mediator.

Responsibility for the situation in Kosovo goes to the top of the Yugoslav government, in the person of Slobodan Milosevic. This person should be indicted for crimes against humanity in Croatia, genocide in Bosnia, and now, atrocities in Kosovo. It is time for the West to stop treating him as "a man we can do business with."

# An Albanian Man Testifies About Serb Atrocities

*Lutfi Ramadani, interviewed by the International Criminal Tribunal for the Former Yugoslavia*

*Lutfi Ramadani is an Albanian man who testified about Serb atrocities in hearings at the International Criminal Tribunal for the Former Yugoslavia (ICTY). The following viewpoint includes excerpts from his testimony, in which he describes how Albanians in his Kosovo village were rounded up and terrorized in March 1999. Ramadani says Serb policemen burned buildings in the village, and the Albanian men were forced into a cowshed, where they were shot. Ramadani explains that he was one of few survivors. He reports that women and children were forced to leave their village and told to go to Albania. Ramadani also testifies that two of his sons were killed in the violence.*

Tove Nilsen, lawyer at the International Criminal Tribunal for the Former Yugoslavia: Mr. Ramadani, if you can tell the Court, prior to March 1999, approximately how was the ethnic distribution in the village Krusha e Vogel? How many houses, approximately, were Albanian, and how many were Serbian?

Lutfi Ramadani: There were 70 Albanian households in Krusha e Vogel. Thirty households were Serbian.

*Thank you. How as far to your knowledge did the different ethnics co-exist before March 1999?*

There was no problem whatsoever between the Albanians and the Serbs. There was nothing wrong in the relations between the Serbs and the Albanians. . . .

*You have told previously that you were more than 500 people who fled into the woods the 25th and that you heard firing from the village that you had fled from. What happened to the people who remained in the woods and those who did not spend the night at Sejdi Batusha's house, Mr. Ramadani?*

They spent the night in the woods up until the very morning. They had something to eat. They had something to eat, and they were able to survive the night. They were able to listen to what was happening, but they spent the night there in that little creek, around that little creek.

*Do you know how many there were?*

Eight people, two families.

*Can you mention the surname of these two families?*

Liman Hazeri with his wife and their son Avdyl, his brother Nebi, Nebi's wife, and Luan. There were two others who were also in the same company, two children. Avdyl was the one who was disabled, and that is why it was impossible to move him. They carried him on the 26th to get him to where the rest of the population was.

*Thank you. What happened with the people who spent the night in Sejdi Batusha's house? What happened the next morning? What did you observe?*

On the evening of the 25th, we went there because it was very, very cold. There were elderly people, women who had given birth two or three days earlier, and that is the reason why we headed toward Sejdi Batusha's house, where we spent the night. When we woke up on the 26th in the morning, almost the entire population that was there emerged into the courtyard. That is at about 7.00 in the morning. We just observed and listened to what was happening on the outskirts of the village. However, on the 25th and the 26th, shelling resumed on the part of the Serbs of that village, as well as the policemen and the others who had come to their aid. They started setting fire to the houses of the Albanians. Initially they went to the houses to carry out their looting, after which they set fire to the houses. They brought trucks. They filled them up. As soon as the trucks and lorries were on their way, they set fire to the villages, and the fire was approaching the population. At the same time, Isen Kanjusha was killed in his own courtyard by the Serbs and—

*I'll stop you there.*

—the police were in the vicinity. Forgive me.

## Some in Uniforms, Some Not

*Sorry. You said the policemen and the others. Who are these others that you're talking about?*

There were the Serbs from the same village. Some had their uniforms on; some were in civilian clothing. There were others, as well, policemen in uniform who had come all the way from Prizren or from elsewhere. I'm not sure. So they kept approaching the population while setting fire to the properties, and when they approached to Milaim Batusha's house, which is adjacent to Sejdi Batusha's house—I can show that on the map if need be—and then they—in fact, we—we were beginning to get scared because they started removing some tiles from the houses and shooting from there. On Milaim Batusha's house, they just opened the windows on the first floor and put the automatic rifles through, and they observed us. When the women saw that had they killed Isen, some of them—some from amongst the women started fainting. There were quite a few who went to fetch some water when they heard from the windows the order not to move, not to go to fetch any water on pain of death, which meant that nobody was able to move, and we had to stand still. And we only used the water that was available to pour onto their faces.

*Okay. I want to know, when you were inside Sejdi Batusha's house, did you have any discussion with each other, what to do? Did you hear about any arrangements that had been made previously that maybe affected on what you did next?*

Others were involved in—in talking what to do. I wasn't involved. We heard that there was some sort of talks between Albanians and Serbs, but I myself was not personally present, and I don't know what happened. I think there was some elderly gentlemen who were involved. They have since departed. But I personally am not aware of what kind of talks they had. Whatever agreement they were able to reach, however, was never—was never observed by the Serbs.

## Killed in His Own Courtyard

*Thank you. Can you please describe what happened next? You are—you have already told that you saw a man being killed, and you named this person. Can you please mention it again?*

Isen Kanjusha, who was killed in his own courtyard, which is adjacent to the house of Sejdi Batusha. We were able to see him being killed from the courtyard of Sejdi Batusha's house, and that is the reason why women and men and everybody got scared. Police came and established themselves in Milaim's house, which added to the fear amongst the children and the women and the men that were over there.

*Thank you. At some stage, you were gathered together with the people who had spent the night in the woods. In which way did this happen? How were you gathered together, and can you please tell the Court what happened then when you [were] there together in the yard?*

Do you mean [when] we were in that courtyard or when we were in the woods?

*I mean when you were in this courtyard and the people from the woods afterwards gathered together with you.*

Okay. I understand it now. When we were ordered not to move to go and fetch water, they called for a volunteer to go to them. Aziz Shehu went, and he was ordered—he was given ten minutes to go and summon the people who were up in the mountains to come down. Aziz went.

As I said, it was Liman Hazeri, and they carried Avdyl and brought him to join the rest of the people there, and as soon as that happened we were ordered to move out of the courtyard and onto the road but to leave everything behind, clothes, everything, and just go out into the road.

*Thank you. Could you please describe, Mr. Ramadani, who these people were that were giving you and the other women, everyone these orders? Can you describe them?*

Policemen. They were policemen.

*And can you just describe briefly their uniforms, how you were seeing them? Were they wearing weapons, and which kind of weapons?*

Blue uniforms, while their weapons—they had automatic weapons and pistols and knives, everything that the policemen usually have as weapons. There, all of them were policemen, while the army, they were along the asphalt road and on the hills.

## Men and Women Separated

*Thank you. And when you were then separated from the women and brought to this barn, the cow-shed, do you remember anything from the walk down the road, who you were walking next to and what you saw?*

We remained on the road for some time until they separated the men from the women. They told the women to leave in the direction to the left and told us to go in the direction to the right. The women set off. Cvetkovic Djordje, a policeman, ordered two other policemen to go and fetch the other children who were up to the age of 13 and bring them where the men were. So these two policemen went to get the children, but the women couldn't let their children go. They started to use force. The women started screaming and yelling, and they told them to shut up and threatened to kill them all.

So they asked them, What are we supposed to do now? You took our men. You took our children. And they said to them, You can go and drown yourself in the Drini River or you can go to Albania. You make your choice.

So after they separated the women, we were told to kneel down and to put our hands over our heads. We stayed in that position for some time. Then some policemen came. They were dressed in uniforms and wore balaklavas [ski masks]. They maltreated us for some time. We remained there for some time again. They took all our money and documents. They told us to empty our pockets. They told Adem Jusufi to collect all the items that we took from our pockets and bring them to one of the policemen. So then they ordered us to stand up and to form columns of three and to walk along the road.

When they went to take the children from the women, my young son, who was 13, was one who was brought in. . . .

## The Cattle Barn

So we were walking along the road, and when we arrived at Qazim Batusha's house they ordered us to stop. They took us directly to the barn. This barn had walls, concrete blocks. There was fodder for the cattle there. The owner used to keep the cattle inside there in the past, but he didn't at the time when we were taken in. . . .

One hundred and nine men were forced into this location. There were two invalids, but the one with the wheelchair is Sait Hajdari. Avdyl was carried inside the barn, while the one who was in the wheelchair, he remained at the door.

After a short time, the policemen came—it didn't take them that long—and they started to shoot inside the location. I saw a policeman who was wearing a helmet, who was wearing uniform, and others joined in in the shooting with automatic rifles, machine-guns, some from the windows, some from the door, and they were shooting at us.

When they finished all the rounds, they came in and with their pistols, whoever would lift his head up, they would shoot them with a pistol. Later on, I didn't see how, but we were caught in fire. Everything was on fire, the bodies, the walls. So when the location was set on fire, my hand, this one got burned. My clothes were—parts of them were burning because I was covered by other bodies.

When I reached the door, Sait Hajdari was there in his wheelchair. I just pushed him a little bit so I could make a leave-way for me, and the room was filled with smoke and fire.

I managed to came—come out. There were people outside here, policemen and other people here on this road. I didn't have time to see who that was. I just escaped here to the left and through our houses.

I left 103 men behind, four of them my family members, two of my sons, that is, and my brother and his son.

# A Ten-Year-Old Albanian Boy Loses His Family to Serb Violence

*Associated Press*

*The Associated Press (AP) is an international news service. In the following viewpoint, the AP reports on Dren Caka, a ten-year-old Albanian boy who was wounded by Serb forces. The author explains that Caka's family was found hiding in a basement by Serb forces. The Serbs opened fire, killing Caka's mother and three sisters and wounding Caka in the arm. The author relates that Caka escaped and found family members, who then drove across the border into Albania. Caka was evacuated by helicopter to a hospital for treatment of his arm. The author also discusses the crowded and desperate conditions in the refugee camps and notes that many other refugees have been wounded as well.*

Kukes, Albania (AP)—Ten-year-old Dren Caka fingers the inflatable brace wrapped around his bullet-shattered right arm and asks, "Will it move again?"

"Of course," a doctor assures the boy as she pumps antibiotics into the IV drip hanging by a wire paper clip. They are in a tidy Italian field clinic in the center of a chaotic refugee camp swelling by the hour with more tractors, cars and horse-drawn wagons.

*Dren Caka, seen in this photo sitting with his father Ali, explains that he pretended to be dead to survive a massacre by Serb forces in Kosovo.* © AP Images/Hektor Pustina.

Dren says he was shot as Serb police slaughtered his family. His arm, too damaged to carry his 2-year-old sister to safety from a burning home, festered and dripped a trail of blood throughout a two-day journey to Albania.

The thumb-size hole above his elbow will heal. But a scar will remind him forever of the brutality in Kosovo that has destroyed families, leveled towns, overwhelmed aid groups. And left one brown-haired boy bravely trying not to cry or think too much about what now lies ahead.

The yellow Yugo reaches the border post late Monday afternoon. Dren's uncle is driving. Dren is in the back seat with his young cousins, his arm cushioned by bloody pieces of bed sheets.

Doctors are waiting. Other refugees have told them of a badly wounded boy back in the line of traffic stretching more than 12 miles.

"Come on, move!" shouts Dr. Flori Bakalli, a Kosovo refugee who took up with the French group Doctors of the World a few days ago.

The sling is removed. Blood spurts from the wound. Dren winces as medics squirt iodine over his arm.

"Courage, courage," Bakalli says.

Dren whimpers, then grows quiet as anesthesia brings relief.

As doctors work, his relatives help the boy tell his story.

It begins before dawn Saturday when they claim Yugoslav police began looting and burning homes on Milos Gjlic street in Djakovica, in southern Kosovo.

"They were howling like wolves," says his uncle, Selajdin Dylhasi.

Dren and 19 women and children, including his mother and three sisters, hide in a basement. But they are quickly discovered and accused of being supporters of the Kosovo Liberation Army, the ethnic Albanian separatists fighting the forces of Yugoslav President Slobodan Milosevic.

A 13-year-old girl is shot first, Dren says. Then, one by one, the police lower their guns and fire. It takes less than a minute.

"I was hit in the arm, but I fell and pretended I was dead," the boy says.

The police set the home ablaze and move on, he says. Thinking everyone is dead, he starts to run. Then he hears moans from his baby sister.

"I tried to pick her up, but . . . but . . . ." Dren says before breaking into tears and pointing to his arm.

His uncle takes over: "He means he couldn't lift her because of his arm. She burned to death in the house."

Dren stumbles to a relative's house. They gather other family members and head for the border, about 16 miles by road.

The surviving clan includes Dren's four grandparents, two aunts, an uncle and two cousins. Dren's father had fled to the mountains with other men from the village. They last heard he, too, has made it over the border.

"He has only his son left," says Dren's 68-year-old grandfather, Xhemal Caka. "Maybe he will join the KLA and seek revenge. That's what I would do if I was younger."

Dren, too young to fight, looks over to his grandfather.

"Maybe someday I will be the one to kill Milosevic," the boy says.

Dren wakes Tuesday with his aunt, Nimete Babalia, stroking his forehead and cowlicked hair. She still wears the corduroy slippers she fled in.

"You're going on a helicopter today," she says. "They are taking you to a big hospital."

To one side of Dren's bed, a woman vomits watery green bile. An old man on another cot wheezes and shakes. He is too ill to tell doctors what's wrong. Outside, a line of people forms. One woman is bent in pain from the infected incision of a Caesarean section two days before. Her husband cradles their crying newborn boy.

A French doctor, Anne Marie Guilleux, pushes through the tent flaps to Dren's section. First, she looks in on a 4-year-old boy whose calf was blown off by mortar fire.

Then she pulls back the yellow blankets covering Dren.

"Good," she says as she looks at his arm and presses his chest, covered by an undershirt that is stiff and rusty-colored with dried blood. Drops of blood dot his pants and blue-stripped socks.

The doctor leaves for other patients, and Dren's 6-year-old cousin, Vjosa, slips him some chocolate and kisses his forehead. They smile at each other.

"Grandfather?" Dren asks. "Wherever we go, do you think they will play soccer there as well?"

Xhemal Caka nods comfortingly. He doesn't want to tell the boy they have no idea what will happen to them. Like almost every refugee, they were stripped of all money and documents.

"We have only God's mercy," says grandfather Caka.

# Serbian Sisters Report on Living Through the NATO Bombing

*Ivanka and Olga Besevic*

*Ivanka Besevic is a retired Belgrade journalist; Olga Besevic is her sister. The following viewpoint is a diary of the Besevic sisters' experiences during the NATO (North Atlantic Treaty Organization) bombing of Serbia. The sisters talk about the constant terror of waiting for NATO bombs to fall, and they report on extensive civilian casualties. They speculate that the NATO planes deliberately targeted civilians to terrorize the population. They argue that the bombing would not bring peace but would instead radicalize right-wing groups in Serbia. After the cessation of bombing, they say that the attacks did not result in peace in Kosovo. Instead, they maintain, Kosovo has been plunged into chaos, with widespread violence committed by Albanians bent on revenge against Serbs.*

I am Ivanka Besevic, a 74-year-old retired journalist from Belgrade [the capital of Serbia]. My daughter, Silvia Miller, who lives in San Francisco, asked me to write to her daily about my life with my sister Olga and our survival during the NATO

[North Atlantic Treaty Organization] bombing of Belgrade. She published my e-mail letters and phone calls on the Internet daily while Yugoslavia was under attack. This diary, "Keep Faith," was never intended to be an impartial record. It would be impossible for me to do so while my own country is getting blown to pieces and my friends are getting older and sicker under never-ending sirens. From the letters sent to me by some who have viewed the website, I know that a few letter writers are angry at me because I don't write more about the Kosovo coverage, or Albanian refugees,[1] and show a side of the war they don't have a chance to see on CNN. It's my family's personal decision to publish my thoughts: to keep us all busy and give us a sense of purpose in this insanity; to keep a loving record in the case of something bad happening; to process the terror and forget for a moment our fears for each other.

I tell about the things I see, feel, and experience, and the things that happen to my family and friends. If I were living in Kosovo, I'd be writing about it, and my experiences there. The refugees I meet on my doorsteps, however, are only the ones that arrive here. They are of all nationalities (there are quite a few Albanian and Roma [Gypsy] refugees in Belgrade too), but they have never stayed in a refugee camp in Albania and don't know about life in it. Knowing that there are so many interested in more knowledge about our disaster is a very hopeful sign for all of us here.

## March 24 [1999]

*Ivanka* We found out that the nearest shelter is fifteen minutes away. There was no way that we could get to it—the defense says that we have only nine seconds to get somewhere when the sirens start. Besides, Olga refused to leave Timmy, and they don't allow pets in the shelters, it's too crowded. I can't say that I blamed her. . . . Olga and I worked on cleaning up the basement of my apartment building and converting it into a shelter for us and the neighborhood children. It's scary and dark in there, as there is only one entrance and no windows. . . .

*Olga* I am worried. You never know when the air-raid is going to start. . . . The worst of all is the terrible speed with which everything happens. I hear detonations, start running home to the basement, the sirens start wailing, and everything is happening in slow motion—except for the bombs coming fast, very fast. The whole war is almost surreal, a video game. Half the time we pretend that nothing's happening; city transportation is running better than ever, driven by volunteer drivers, and concert halls and theaters are giving free performances to all who want to see them. Other times, we are running to turn off all the lights and sit in the dark, underground, waiting to die.

## April 7

*Ivanka* I sleep well, but Olga rarely shuts her eyes before dawn. Hearing the growl of the bombs in the dark is still better than the silence—at least we know that they are far away; the anticipation of waking up in the fires of a man-made hell is much worse. We cope. During the day, everyone goes to work, the stores are open, doctors heal, artists create beauty. Then, as the night approaches, we scatter to our darkened holes, usually in groups. This will teach us a hard lesson in humanity. We watched the massacres in other parts of the world, always thinking, "We are a civilized country; a thing like that could never happen here—the homeless, the hungry, sicknesses this continent hasn't seen since the holding pens of German occupation." Now people die in concentration camps, not in Yugoslavia, but in the cannibal alliance trying to devour it. All the atrocities that the nationalist Serbs have committed, and all the horrors that the terrorist KLA [Kosovo Liberation Army] have wrought pale by comparison. Are they trying to show us what *real* atrocities are, so we would hang our heads in shame for our petty terrorism and all get along, dead or alive?

## May 1

*Ivanka* We were spared last night, but had no rest nevertheless. There was such a storm that we were not able to tell the thunder and lightning from the bombs. At this point we are so jumpy that we leap into the air at any sudden noise—both from the lack of sleep and the realization that the gloves are off and NATO really wants us dead, all of us. It was a strange storm that started with the first sirens (the entire day was sunny and quite warm), blasted through the night, and died out with the morning and the end of the air danger. We are spread so widely around our poor violated country that there is always an eyewitness account to anything that happens. The downside is that, wherever the Bombing du Jour happens, we have to fear for our loved ones. I don't care for myself: I am old and had a full, wonderfully fulfilled life. I am angry because of the children screaming in nightmares of bombing, because of a generation sentenced to grow up in poisons (fishing in the Danube [River] is now banned—the water is deadly), sentenced to starve because their parents' workplaces are now bomb craters. Sentenced to live in shame of their nationality being linked to the worst crimes, with no proof. I am angry because of having money taken from my every paycheck, my entire working life of forty years, to fund the development of Kosovo, just to see NATO bomb all that we built into dust—so that no one, not Serbs or Albanians, will ever have any use of it.

## May 16

*Olga* It's really hard to figure out where to be safe. The people living near the most obvious targets stay with family or friends in the more innocuous areas, just as Ivanka does, living with me now. There are several "legitimate targets" up and down the street from my apartment, but at least we are not next to Yugoslavia's biggest newspaper, where Ivanka's home is. My friend Danka, who lives on the second floor nearby, says that as soon as the sirens start, she goes to one room of her apartment that has no apartment over it on the third floor—just the roof. She's terrified of being buried and crashed by concrete from the floors above her, and afraid of having to live mutilated or as an amputee, so she counts on a quick death by exposing herself to a direct hit, if there is one. Even the children are trying to process what goes on in their own way. I heard a new version of the Red Riding Hood story told by a little girl, in which Red Riding Hood's parents warn her not to talk to strangers in the forest, as well as to run and hide if she hears the sirens start. One of my violin students said that they call a feared biology teacher "Madame Albright."[2]

## June 1

*Ivanka* Ah, we are starting another month of war, with bigger and better bombs, and more carpet bombing than ever. In the last three days, they hit point blank a bridge full of people during a major religious holiday, Pentecost, and Sunday market crowds (casualties included a priest and many others who came in to help after the first wave); also hit were a hospital, an old folks home, a convoy of foreign journalists, and now the apartment building in Novi Pazar. Dozens and dozens of dead—the old, the sick, and children. The bombers have been returning after the first hits to bomb the relief workers and good Samaritans, too. Surdulica, where the hospital and old folks home were hit, has only 12,000 people living in it. By the time everyone is killed, they'd have spent a bomb for each person dying in there. What really chills me is the thought that the bombing really *is* a success, as they are stating—that they are doing exactly what they intended when destroying the cities and people and children like this. I believe this is correct. All of us who are being bombed here—who can smell the air rushing from the bomb hits and see the dead bodies—think the same. We are here, and we see it with our own eyes: every civilian target, our neighbors' homes. They are still counting the bodies. . . .

## June 12–16

*Olga* I am sleeping a bit better, but still have some troubles. It's so quiet—with no bombs and no Ivanka.[3]

I despise nationalism of all kinds, and this atmosphere is more and more conducive to it. During all these years of sanctions and the breakup of the country, it was natural, but not excusable, that some would turn to nationalism—usually the loudest ones. What to expect now, after the country has been bombed into the Middle Ages, but the strengthening of the medieval attitudes. Even the most moderate factions are turning strongly to the religious right of some kind; and what is going to happen now, if there *is* an election? The ruling party is not the most nationalistic party, not by far. War never has brought moderation. Many of the Serbs who had no grudge against the Albanians are now—now that they have lost their own homes and children to bombing—hateful of them. Kosovo is a terrible, terrible mess! Serbs, Gypsies, and other ethnicities, as well as the Albanians who were against secession—people are now running in thousands (from 15,000 to 30,000, according to different sources) in the three days we have had peace. The KLA is burning and pillaging Serb houses, and it has not been demilitarized at all, as NATO was supposed to insist on according to the signed peace accord. I can only suppose that there's a lot of burning being done the other way around too (not much of that in papers here)—by the retreating paramilitary and people. I heard reports of Serbs burning their own houses and those of their neighbors in order to leave nothing to the advancing enemy. . . . It doesn't matter anymore. We are all so tired. Nobody won, except for the bomb-makers.

## July 5

*Olga* I spoke again with [our friend] Zivka, and she said it's still war in Kosovo. Her family was forced out. Their cows are loose and dying without people to take care of them, and they lost all they ever had. It's chaos down there. There are gangs all over the place. What the papers are saying—that the province is getting more peaceful—is plain untruth. . . . Another one of my friends, an army electric repairman who recently returned from Kosovo, was very, very serious when he told me that it's not over, that it's complete destruction and chaos in the south, and that he would not be surprised if our whole country goes up in flames. Everyone expects the continuation of war in August. I haven't removed the protective tape from my windows. No one else is pretending that the war is over either. It's true only for the safe countries that have the luxury to select soldiers, not civilians, to be sent to die. War is all around us here, in power struggles, rubble, and guns.

## Notes

1. Serbian efforts to suppress ethnic Albanian independence movements in Kosovo were followed by atrocities against Albanians. NATO bombed Serbia to end the violence in Kosovo.
2. This is a reference to US Secretary of State Madeleine Albright, an advocate of the NATO bombing.
3. Ivanka Besevic is with her daughter, Silvia, in San Francisco at this point.

# Glossary

**Albanians** An ethnic group concentrated in the country of Albania and the neighboring Kosovo. Albanians speak the Albanian language and are mostly Muslim.

**Bosnia-Herzegovina** A country that was once part of Yugoslavia. Bosnia-Herzegovina declared itself independent from Yugoslavia in the early 1990s, prompting a war with Serbia and Croatia that ended in 1995.

**Croatia** A country that was once part of Yugoslavia. It declared independence in 1991, resulting in a war with Serbia that lasted until 1995.

**Kosovo Liberation Army (KLA)** A Kosovar Albanian organization that used violence and terrorism to try to force Serbia to grant independence to Kosovo. Its actions, and the resulting Serbian crackdown, helped precipitate the Kosovo War of 1998–1999.

**Roma (or Romani)** An ethnic group, sometimes known as Gypsies, who live throughout Europe. They have often faced discrimination.

**Serbia** A country that was once part of Yugoslavia. Its population is more than 80% Serbs, who are predominantly Orthodox Christian.

**Yugoslavia** A socialist federation composed of Serbia, Croatia, Kosovo, and other provinces. Yugoslavia was created after World War II and lasted until communism collapsed in Eastern Europe in 1991.

# Organizations to Contact

*The editors have compiled the following list of organizations concerned with the issues debated in this book. The descriptions are derived from materials provided by the organizations. All have publications or information available for interested readers. The list was compiled on the date of publication of the present volume; the information provided here may change. Be aware that many organizations take several weeks or longer to respond to inquiries, so allow as much time as possible.*

**Amnesty International**
5 Penn Plaza
New York, NY 10001
(212) 807-8400 • fax: (212) 463-9193
e-mail: aimember@aiusa.org
website: www.amnestyusa.org

Amnesty International is a worldwide movement of people who campaign for internationally recognized human rights. Its vision is of a world in which every person enjoys all of the human rights enshrined in the Universal Declaration of Human Rights and other international human rights standards. Each year the organization publishes a report on its work and its concerns throughout the world. Amnesty International's website includes numerous reports and news items about the status of the Roma in Kosovo, as well as other issues relating to human rights in Kosovo.

**Carnegie Endowment for International Peace (CEIP)**
1779 Massachusetts Ave. NW
Washington, DC 20036
(202) 483-7600 • fax: (202) 483-1840
e-mail: info@ceip.org
website: www.ceip.org

This private, nonprofit organization is dedicated to advancing cooperation between nations and promoting active international engagement by the United States. It publishes the quarterly journal *Foreign Policy*, a magazine of international politics and economics that is published in several languages and reaches readers in more than 120 countries. Its website includes numerous news articles and publications, including "Cut the Gordian Knot in Kosovo" and *Intervention in Internal Conflicts: Legal and Political Conundrums.*

**Gendercide Watch**
Suite #501, 10011 - 116th Street
Edmonton, Alberta, Canada T5K 1V4
e-mail: office@gendercide.org
website: www.gendercide.org

Gendercide Watch seeks to confront acts of gender-selective mass killing around the world. It works to raise awareness of such acts and to reduce stereotypes and reprisals against victims. Gendercide Watch conducts research, provides educational resources, and maintains a website. The website includes an extensive series of cases studies, news releases, and other information pertaining to gendercide.

**Human Rights Watch**
350 Fifth Ave., 34th Floor
New York, NY 10118-3299
(212) 290-4700 • fax: (212) 736-1300
e-mail: hrwnyc@hrw.org
website: www.hrw.org

Founded in 1978, this nongovernmental organization conducts systematic investigations of human rights abuses in countries around the world. It opposes discrimination against those with HIV/AIDS. It publishes many books and reports on specific countries and issues as well as annual reports and other articles. Its website includes numerous discussions of human rights and international justice issues as they relate to Kosovo.

## Institute for the Study of Genocide (ISG)
John Jay College of Criminal Justice
899 Tenth Ave., Room 325
New York, NY 10019
e-mail: info@instituteforthestudyofgenocide.org
website: www.instituteforthestudyofgenocide.org

The ISG is an independent nonprofit organization that promotes and disseminates scholarship and policy analyses on the causes, consequences, and prevention of genocide. To advance these ends, it publishes a semiannual newsletter and working papers; holds periodic conferences; maintains liaisons with academic, human rights, and refugee organizations; provides consultation to representatives of media, governmental, and nongovernmental organizations; and advocates passage of legislation and administrative measures related to genocide and gross violations of human rights. In addition to newsletters, the ISG publishes books on the topic of genocide such as *Ever Again?: Evaluating the United Nations Genocide Convention on Its 50th Anniversary and Proposals to Activate the Convention* and *The Prevention of Genocide: Rwanda and Yugoslavia Reconsidered.*

## International Criminal Court (ICC)
PO Box 19519
2500 CM, The Hague, The Netherlands
31 (0)70 515 8515 • fax: 31 (0)70 515 8555
e-mail: visit@icc-cpi.int
website: www.icc-cpi.int

The ICC is a treaty-based international court established to try the perpetrators of the most serious crimes in the international community. Its website includes annual reports on the activities of the court, information about situations and cases, relevant legal texts, and other information.

**Montreal Institute for Genocide and Human Rights Studies (MIGS)**
Concordia University
1455 De Maisonneuve Boulevard West
Montreal, Quebec, Canada H3G 1M8
(514) 848-2424 ext. 5729 or 2404 • fax: (514) 848-4538
website: http://migs.concordia.ca

MIGS, founded in 1986, monitors native language media for early warning signs of genocide in countries deemed to be at risk of mass atrocities. The institute houses the Will to Intervene (W2I) Project, a research initiative focused on the prevention of genocide and other mass atrocity crimes. The institute also collects and disseminates research on the historical origins of mass killings and provides comprehensive links to this and other research materials on its website.

**North Atlantic Treaty Organization (NATO)**
Boulevard Leopold III
1110 Brussels, Belgium
website: www.nato.int

NATO is an intergovernmental military alliance including the United States and many European nations. It safeguards the safety and freedom of member countries through military and political means. Its website includes news releases, speeches, transcripts, and other information, including many documents relating to NATO's involvement in Kosovo.

**Prevent Genocide International (PGI)**
1804 S Street NW
Washington, DC 20009

(202) 483-1948 • fax: (202) 328-0627
e-mail: info@preventgenocide.org
website: www.preventgenocide.org

PGI is a global education and action network established in 1998 with the purpose of bringing about the elimination of the crime of genocide. In an effort to promote education on the subject of genocide, PGI maintains a multilingual website to educate the international community, particularly targeting those nations not yet belonging to the United Nations Genocide Convention. The website maintains a database of government documents and news releases, as well as original content provided by members.

**STAND/United to End Genocide**
1025 Connecticut Ave., Suite 310
Washington, DC 20036
(202) 556-2100
e-mail: info@standnow.org
website: www.standnow.org

STAND is the student-led division of United to End Genocide (formerly Genocide Intervention Network). STAND envisions a world in which the global community is willing and able to protect civilians from genocide and mass atrocities. In order to empower individuals and communities with the tools to stop genocide, STAND recommends activities from engaging government representatives to hosting fundraisers and has more than one thousand student chapters at colleges and high schools. While maintaining many documents online regarding genocide, STAND provides a plan to promote action as well as education.

**United Human Rights Council (UHRC)**
104 North Belmont Street, Suite 313
Glendale, CA 91206
(818) 507-1933
website: www.unitedhumanrights.org

The United Human Rights Council (UHRC) is a committee of the Armenian Youth Federation. By means of action on a grass-roots level the UHRC works toward exposing and correcting human rights violations of governments worldwide. The UHRC campaigns against violators in an effort to generate awareness through boycotts, community outreach, and education. The UHRC website focuses on the genocides of the twentieth century.

**United States Department of State**
2201 C Street NW
Washington, DC 20520
(202) 647-4000
website: www.state.gov

The US Department of State is the agency of the federal government responsible for foreign affairs. Its website includes daily press briefings, reports on policy issues, and numerous other articles. The site includes fact sheets and other information about Kosovo.

# List of Primary Source Documents

*The editors have compiled the following list of documents that either broadly address genocide and persecution or more narrowly focus on the topic of this volume. The full text of these documents is available from multiple sources in print and online.*

**Congressional Record, March 22, 1999**

A record of the US Senate debate on whether to authorize force against Serbia.

**Convention Against Torture and Other Cruel, Inhuman or Degrading Treatment or Punishment**
**United Nations, 1974**

A draft resolution adopted by the United Nations General Assembly in 1974 opposing any nation's use of torture, unusually harsh punishment, and unfair imprisonment.

**Convention on the Prevention and Punishment of the Crime of Genocide, December 9, 1948**

A resolution of the United Nations General Assembly that defines genocide in legal terms and advises participating countries to prevent and punish actions of genocide in war and peacetime.

**Indictment by the International Criminal Tribunal for the Former Yugoslavia (ICTY) Against Yugoslav Leaders, May 22, 1999**

An indictment against Serbian officials, including leader Slobodan Milosevic, for crimes against humanity in Kosovo, including deportation, murder, and persecutions. The treaty provided Kosovo with a great degree of autonomy but was rejected by Yugoslavia, prompting NATO to start the Kosovo War.

## Interim Agreement for Peace and Self-Government in Kosovo (Rambouillet Agreement), February 23, 1999

The proposed NATO peace agreement between ethnic Albanians in Kosovo and then-Yugoslavia.

## Principles of International Law Recognized in the Charter of the Nuremburg Tribunal
## United Nations International Law Commission, 1950

After World War II (1939–1945) the victorious allies legally tried surviving leaders of Nazi Germany in the German city of Nuremburg. The proceedings established standards for international law that were affirmed by the United Nations and by later court tests. Among other standards, national leaders can be held responsible for crimes against humanity, which might include "murder, extermination, deportation, enslavement, and other inhuman acts."

## Report of United Nations Secretary General Annan to the President of the United Nations Security Council, November 12, 1998

A report on the military and humanitarian situation in Kosovo in 1998, including recommendations for UN actions.

## Rome Statute of the International Criminal Court, July 17, 1998

The treaty that established the International Criminal Court. It establishes the court's functions, jurisdiction, and structure.

## United Nations General Assembly Resolution 96 on the Crime of Genocide, December 11, 1946

A resolution of the United Nations General Assembly that affirms that genocide is a crime under international law.

## United Nations Security Council Resolution 1244, June 10, 1999

A resolution that authorized an international civil and military presence in Kosovo. It effectively provided for peace between Serbia and Kosovo and the conclusion of the military conflict.

## Universal Declaration of Human Rights
## United Nations, 1948

Soon after its founding, the United Nations approved this general statement of individual rights it hoped would apply to citizens of all nations.

## Whitaker Report on Genocide, 1985

This report addresses the question of the prevention and punishment of the crime of genocide. It calls for the establishment of an international criminal court and a system of universal jurisdiction to ensure that genocide is punished.

# For Further Research

## Books

Alastair Finlan, *The Collapse of Yugoslavia 1991–1999*. Oxford, UK: Osprey, 2004.

Janine di Giovanni, *Madness Visible: A Memoir of War*. New York: Random House, 2003.

Ian F. Hancock, *We Are the Romani People: Volume 28*. Hertfordshire, AL: Hertfordshire Press, 2002.

Tim Judah, *Kosovo: War and Revenge*, 2nd ed. New Haven, CT: Yale Nota Bene, 2002.

Tim Judah, *The Serbs: History, Myth and the Destruction of Yugoslavia*, 3rd ed. New Haven, CT: Yale University Press, 2010.

Philip Kearney, *Under the Blue Flag: My Mission in Kosovo*. Beverly Hills, CA: Phoenix Books, 2008.

Iain King and Whit Mason, *Peace at Any Price: How the World Failed Kosovo*. Ithaca, NY: Cornell University Press, 2006.

Julie A. Mertus, *Kosovo: How Myths and Truths Started a War*. Berkeley: University of California Press, 1999.

Norman M. Naimark, *Fires of Hatred: Ethnic Cleansing in Twentieth-Century Europe*. Cambridge, MA: Harvard University Press, 2002.

James Pettifer and Miranda Vickers, *The Albanian Question: Reshaping the Balkans*. New York: I.B. Tauris, 2007.

Dale C. Tatum, *Genocide at the Dawn of the Twenty-First Century: Rwanda, Bosnia, Kosovo, and Darfur*. New York: Palgrave Macmillan, 2010.

## Periodicals and Internet Sources

Alexei G. Arbatov, "The Kosovo Crisis: The End of the Post–Cold War Era," The Atlantic Council of the United States, March 2000. http://ics.leeds.ac.uk.

BBC News, "Kosovo Assault 'Was Not Genocide,'" September 7, 2001. http://news.bbc.co.uk.

Theo Brinkel, "Kosovo and the Just War Tradition," *Public Justice Report*, Center for Public Justice, Third Quarter 1999. www.cpjustice.org.

Noam Chomsky, "A Review of NATO's War Over Kosovo," *Z Magazine,* April–May 2001.

David Clark, "Kosovo Was a Just War, Not an Imperialist Dress Rehearsal," *Guardian*, April 16, 2003. www.guardian.co.uk.

Anna Clarkson, "Six Stories from Kosovo," Mercy Corps, February 25, 2008. www.mercycorps.org.

*Economist,* "The Lessons of Milosevic: Coddling Monsters Has a Price," March 16, 2006. www.economist.com.

*Economist,* "The Roots of the Kosovo Calamity," April 13, 2000. www.economist.com.

William Finnegan, "Letter from Kosovo: The Countdown," *New Yorker,* October 15, 2007. www.newyorker.com.

David N. Gibbs, "Kosovo: A Template for Disaster," *Guardian,* March 21, 2011. www.guardian.co.uk.

Human Rights Watch, "Kosovo/Albania: Investigate Alleged KLA Crimes," December 15, 2010. www.hrw.org.

Human Rights Watch, "Kosovo: Europe Returning Roma to Face Hardship," October 28, 2010. www.hrw.org.

Tim Judah, "History, Bloody History," BBC News, March 24, 1999. http://news.bbc.co.uk.

John Kifner, "Horror by Design: The Ravaging of Kosovo," *New York Times,* June 3, 1999.

Henry H. Perritt Jr., "Kosovo's New Republic," *New Kosovo Report,* February 21, 2008. www.newkosovareport.com.

Carla Del Ponte, interviewed by *Der Spiegel,* "Spiegel Interview with War Crimes Prosecutor Carla Del Ponte: 'Politics Have Interfered with Our Work,'" *Der Spiegel,* October 18, 2007. www.spiegel.de.

Ken Silverstein and Sebastian Sosman, "Kosovo: Mission Accomplished?," *Harper's,* September 15, 2006. http://harpers.org.

Javier Solana, "NATO's Success in Kosovo," *Foreign Affairs,* November/December 1999. www.foreignaffairs.com.

*Der Spiegel,* "A German Soldier Returns to Kosovo: 'So Much Hate and Rage,'" March 25, 2009. www.spiegel.de.

WomenforWomen.org, "Stories from Women: Kosovo." www.womenforwomen.org.

## Other

**The Gypsies of Kosovo: Center for Holocaust and Genocide Studies: University of Minnesota** (http://chgs.umn.edu/educational/gypsies). This website is devoted to a survey of Gypsy (Roma) communities. The website includes a discussion of the Kosovo Roma's history and life after the Kosovo War.

**International Criminal Tribunal for the Former Yugoslavia (ICTY)** (www.icty.org). The International Criminal Tribunal for the Former Yugoslavia is a United Nations court of law dealing with war crimes that took place during the conflicts in the Balkans in the 1990s. Its website includes legal documents, transcripts, reports, press releases, news updates, and more.

**Republic of Kosovo: The Office of the Prime Minister** (www
.kryeministri-ks.net). The website of the office of the elected
leader of the independent Republic of Kosovo includes
news, transcripts of speeches, statements, documents, and
more.

**Serbia Government** (www.srbija.gov.rs). The website of the
Serbian government includes news reports, speeches, and
numerous other documents.

# Index

Scotland, 134
Self interest, 13
Serbia
    Bosnia and, 28
    GDP, 135, 137
    Kosovo humanitarian disaster
      and, 84–92
    Kosovo refugees and, 32
    Muslim Turks (Ottomans) and,
      25
    secret police, 42
    Yugoslavia formation and, 39
    *See also* Kosovo; Milosevic,
      Slobodan; Yugoslavia
Serbian Orthodox Church, 60
Seselj, Vojislav, 149
Sexual violence
    Albanian women and, 30–31,
      49, 53, 97, 115
    Bosnia-Herzogevina and, 113
    ethnic cleansing and, 109–115
    forced pregnancy, 7
    gang rapes, 113
    genocide and, 7, 8, 93–94
    Kosovo Liberation Army (KLA)
      and rape, 115
    refugees and, 114
    sanctioned by military officers,
      112–114
Sierra Leone, 8, 141
Single-interest parties, 13
Sirleaf, Ellen Johnson, 142
Slavery, 7
Slovakia, 158
Slovenia, 18, 39, 56, 85, 103
Smith, Adam, 13
Socialist Party of Serbia, 26, 70
Solana, Javier, 55
Soros, George, 117
South Africa, 94, 101n1
South Korea, 106

South Ossetia, 151–152
Spain, 158
St. Laurent, Louis, 137
Stalin, Joseph, 26, 41
Stambolic, Ivan, 146–147
Sterilization, 7
Stevens, Sinclair, 132–138
Suicide, 146
Sweden, 63
Switzerland, 41

**T**
Tanzania, 11
Taylor, Charles, 142
Technogas, 147
Terrorism, 12
Thaçi, Hashim, 61, 157
Thompson CSF, 136
*Time* (magazine), 147
Tito, Josip Broz
    Albanian culture and, 27, 94
    death, 26
    nationalist movements and,
      40–41
    World War II and, 39
Tokyo war crimes trials, 140
Torture, 5, 7
Transdniestria, 151–152
Treaties of London and Bucharest,
    38
Trepca mines, 99, 100, 101
Tribunal for Sierra Leone, 142
Tudjman, Franjo, 103, 105
Turkey, 86
Tutsi, 10–11

**U**
Uganda, 10
Ukraine, 91
United Nations
    Convention on the Prevention
      and Punishment of the Crime
      of Genocide (UNGC), 5, 6